Edge Interactive
Practice Book

TEACHER'S ANNOTATED EDITION

 Hampton-Brown

 NATIONAL GEOGRAPHIC

National Geographic School Publishing
Hampton–Brown
P.O. Box 223220
Carmel, California 93922
800-333-3510
www.NGSP.com

Printed in the United States of America

ISBN 13: 978-0-7362-3540-2
ISBN 10: 0-7362-3540-X

09 10 11 12 13 14 15 16 10 9 8 7

Unit 2

Unit 4

Unit 6

Prepare to Read

▶ The Experiment
▶ Superstitions: The Truth Uncovered

Key Vocabulary

A. How well do you know these words? Circle a rating for each word. Check your understanding of each word by circling *yes* or *no*. Then, complete the sentences. If you are unsure of a word's meaning, refer to the Vocabulary Glossary, page 764, in your student text.

Rating Scale	
1	I have never seen this word before.
2	I am not sure of the word's meaning.
3	I know this word and can teach the word's meaning to someone else.

Key Word	Check Your Understanding	Deepen Your Understanding
1 belief (bu-**lēf**) *noun* **Rating:** 1 2 3	A person's **belief** is always a well-known fact. Yes (No)	It is my strongest belief *Possible response:* that people must stand up for themselves and their families .
2 escape (is-**kāp**) *verb* **Rating:** 1 2 3	You would want to **escape** an ocean filled with hungry sharks. (Yes) No	If I were trapped on a desert island, I would try to escape by *Possible response:* building a raft out of tree trunks .
3 evidence (**e**-vu-dens) *noun* **Rating:** 1 2 3	A written note left at the scene of a crime can be a good piece of **evidence.** (Yes) No	Detectives study pieces of evidence, such as _____ *Possible response:* fingerprints, tire marks, and weapons .
4 experiment (ik-**spair**-u-munt) *noun* **Rating:** 1 2 3	An **experiment** never solves a problem. Yes (No)	An example of an experiment I have performed is _____ *Possible response:* mixing two chemicals to create a reaction .

Key Word	Check Your Understanding	Deepen Your Understanding
⑤ failure (fāl-yur) *noun* **Rating:** **1 2 3**	Everyone likes **failure.** **Yes**　　(**No**)	The worst failure of communication I ever had was _____ *Possible response:* when I did not call my mom to tell her I would be home late _____ _____ .
⑥ misfortune (mis-**for**-chun) *noun* **Rating:** **1 2 3**	A family that loses their home in a storm is experiencing **misfortune.** (**Yes**)　　**No**	I experienced misfortune when *Possible response:* I lost my wallet _____ _____ _____ .
⑦ mistaken (mi-**stā**-kun) *verb* **Rating:** **1 2 3**	It is possible for a woman to be **mistaken** for her identical twin sister. (**Yes**)　　**No**	I am often mistaken for *Possible response:* my twin sister _____ _____ _____ .
⑧ superstition (sü-pur-**sti**-shun) *noun* **Rating:** **1 2 3**	The idea that Friday the 13th is an unlucky day is a common **superstition.** (**Yes**)　　**No**	One superstition I have heard of is *Possible* *response:* stepping on cracks causes bad luck _____ _____ _____ .

B. Use one of the Key Vocabulary words to write about a superstition or powerful belief you have. How does it influence you?

Answers will vary. _____

_____

Before Reading The Experiment

The Experiment
by Martin Raim

LITERARY ANALYSIS: Plot and Setting

The events that happen in a story are the **plot.** The **setting** is where and when the story takes place. The events of the story are affected by the setting.

A. Read the passage below. Look for details that describe the setting and plot. Write them in the chart.

> **Look Into the Text**
>
> There was no way out.
>
> The walls of his cell were built of thick cement blocks. The huge door was made of steel. The floor and ceiling were made of concrete, and there were no windows. The only light came from a light bulb that was covered by a metal shield.
>
> There was no way out, or so it seemed to him.
>
> He had volunteered to be part of a scientific experiment and had been put in the cell to test the cleverness of the human mind. The cell was empty, and he was not allowed to take anything into it. But he had been told that there was one way to escape from the cell, and he had three hours to find it.

Setting	Plot
a cell built of thick cement blocks	A man is put in a cell and given three hours to escape as part of a scientific experiment.
the door is made of steel	
there are no windows	There is no way out.

B. Use the information in the chart to complete the sentence about the plot and setting.

The volunteer might have difficulty   getting out of the cell because it seems like there is no way out.

There are no windows to escape out of, and the door is made of steel.

READING STRATEGY: Preview and Predict

How to PREVIEW AND PREDICT

1. **Preview** Look at the title, pictures, and key words for clues.

2. **Predict** As you read, ask yourself: *What will happen next?*

A. Read the passage. Use the strategies above to preview and predict what will happen next. Then answer the questions below.

> **Look Into the Text**
>
> The shield! The shield around the light bulb! His mind raced. The metal shield could be used as a tool—the tool he needed! He had found the way to escape! He moved under the shield and looked closely at it. One good strong pull would free it, he decided. He reached up, grabbed hold of it, and pulled. But the shield stayed attached to the ceiling. He grabbed the shield again, twisting it as he pulled. He felt it rip free, and he fell to the floor clutching his treasure.
>
> The shield was shaped like a cone and had been fastened to the ceiling by three long metal prongs. These prongs were sharp. But they were not strong enough to cut through steel or concrete or cement.

1. Do you think the volunteer will be able to escape? Why or why not?

   Possible response: No. The one useful tool he finds is not strong enough to cut through steel or concrete.

2. What do you think will happen next?

   Answers will vary.

B. Reread the passage above. Circle the words and ideas that you used to answer the question.

Selection Review The Experiment

EQ **What Influences How You Act?**
Find out how beliefs affect people.

A. In "The Experiment," you found out how a person's beliefs can affect his actions. Complete the chart below.

Cause-and-Effect Chart

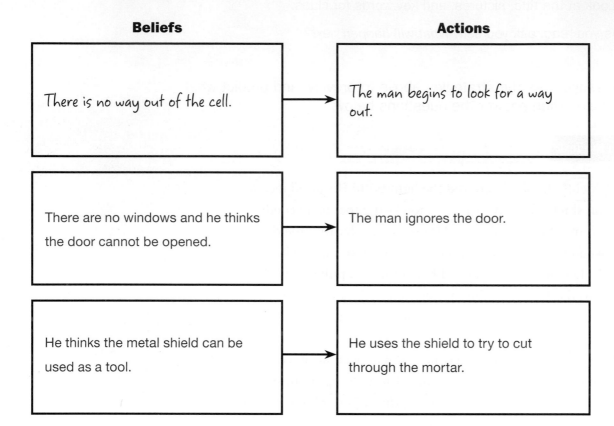

Beliefs	Actions
There is no way out of the cell.	The man begins to look for a way out.
There are no windows and he thinks the door cannot be opened.	The man ignores the door.
He thinks the metal shield can be used as a tool.	He uses the shield to try to cut through the mortar.

B. Use the information you wrote in the chart to answer the questions.

1. Why does the man believe there was no way out of the cell?

There are no windows, and he assumes the steel door is locked.

2. What belief does the man have about himself that may have affected the experiment? Use **belief** in your response.

Possible response: He has the belief that he is clever and that the answer is obvious. In fact, his belief in himself sidetracks him.

3. How might the story be different if there was not a metal shield or light bulb in the cell?

Possible response: The man may have tried pushing on the door to test whether or not it opened.

SUPERSTITIONS:
The Truth Uncovered • by Jamie Kiffel

Connect Across Texts

In "The Experiment," a man's **belief** determines his actions. In this magazine article, find out the truth about some beliefs called **superstitions**.

Some people believe in superstitions to explain **the unexplainable**. Often that means explaining bad luck. Old Mr. Smith's house burned down? He must have forgotten to knock on wood after he said his home **was fireproof**. But where did strange beliefs like this come from, and why did people believe them? Here are the straight facts behind some superstitions.

SUPERSTITION 1
Ravens predict death.

Where It Came From Ravens are **scavengers**, so they were often **spotted** at cemeteries and battlefields—places associated with dying. People started thinking the birds could predict death.

What's the Truth? People who spot ravens could be in for some good luck— not death. According to legend, Vikings sailing the ocean would release **captive ravens** and follow them toward land. If the birds returned, the sailors knew land was still far away. And **tame ravens** are very friendly. "They act like puppies," says Patricia Cole of New York City's Prospect Park Zoo. "They'll sit on your lap, let you scratch their heads, and play tug-of-war!"

The raven became a symbol of death, but some people admire the bird for its intelligence and fearless behavior.

Key Vocabulary
  belief *n.*, something you think is true
  superstition *n.*, an idea based on fear, not science or logic

In Other Words
  the unexplainable things they can't figure out
  was fireproof could not burn down
  scavengers animals that eat dead things
  spotted seen
  captive ravens ravens kept on the ship
  tame ravens ravens that are not wild

Interact with the Text

1. Nonfiction Text Features
Text features such as subtitles provide more information about the content of an article. Underline the main title of the article and the subtitle. How does the subtitle clarify the title?

  The subtitle shows
  that the truth about
  superstitions will be
  uncovered and suggests
  that superstitions might
  not be real, or true.

2. Preview/Set a Purpose
Look at the photos, the caption, and the subheadings. What do you think you will learn about in this section?

  Possible response:
  People think ravens
  predict death because
  of how they look.

3. Nonfiction Text Features
Photos and diagrams support the text. Explain how the diagram, "Triangles in a Doorway," clarifies and supports the text in Superstition 2.

The diagram shows that

a rectangle, or doorway,

is made up of two

triangles.

_____

_____

_____

_____

4. Interpret
Underline the words that explain why people threw salt over their left shoulder. Why was salt so valuable?

Salt was valuable before

there were refrigerators.

Salt preserves food.

_____

_____

_____

_____

_____

_____

_____

_____

SUPERSTITION 2
Walking under a ladder is bad luck.

Where It Came From In ancient times, people believed that triangles were **sacred**. Walking through a triangle could break the triangle's good powers and let evil things **escape**. In this case, the triangle is formed by the ladder and the ground.

What's the Truth? Triangles aren't sacred. They are just three connected points that, unlike the points of a line, aren't in a row. Math experts such as Professor Albert L. Vitter think of rectangular forms—such as doorways—as two triangles. (Picture a line from one corner of a doorway to its diagonal corner.) According to this notion, when you walk through a doorway you are walking through two triangles. Of course, you know by your own experience that it's perfectly safe to do this!

Triangles in a Doorway

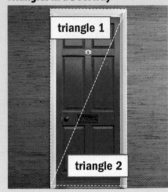

triangle 1

triangle 2

▲ **Interpret the Diagram**
Explain how a doorway is like two triangles.

SUPERSTITION 3
Throwing salt over your left shoulder wards off evil.

Where It Came From In the days before refrigeration, <u>salt was very valuable</u> because people used it to preserve meat, fish, and other foods. <u>People worried that evil spirits might try to steal their salt</u>, especially if it spilled. So they tossed salt over their left shoulders into the eyes of any salt-stealing **demons** to stop them.

Key Vocabulary
escape *v.*, to get free

In Other Words
sacred special, holy
wards off evil keeps away evil
demons bad spirits, devils

What's the Truth? Even if there were really demons, throwing salt in their eyes might slow them down for a little while, but it wouldn't stop them. In fact, salt occurs naturally in tears. <u>It and the proteins in tears keep germs away and help prevent eye infections.</u>

Ninety-eight percent of a tear is water. Tears also contain small amounts of sodium chloride, the chemical name for salt.

5. Interpret
Underline the sentence that describes why salt occurs in tears. What do you think would happen if salt did not occur in tears naturally?

Possible response:

People might have eye

infections.

SUPERSTITION 4
Breaking a mirror means trouble.

Where It Came From People used to believe that your reflection was actually your **soul**. So if you broke a mirror, you'd break—and therefore lose—your soul.

What's the Truth? The image in a mirror is **a phenomenon of** light. "When you look at any object in a mirror, what you're actually seeing is reflected light," says Lou Bloomfield, author of *How Things Work: The Physics of Everyday Life.* When you stand in front of a mirror, reflected light from your body bounces off the mirror's surface. That's why you see your reflection.

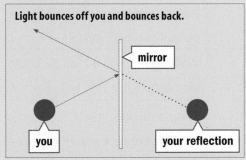

Reflection in a Mirror

Light bounces off you and bounces back.

mirror

you

your reflection

⚠ **Interpret the Diagram** When light from your body hits the surface of the mirror, what happens next? What does this action cause you to see in the mirror?

6. Nonfiction Text Features
In your own words, describe the information in the diagram, "Reflection in a Mirror." Why do you think this diagram was included?

Possible response:

When you look into a

mirror, you see yourself

because light bounces

off you, hits the mirror,

and then bounces

back. The diagram was

included to clarify a

confusing idea.

In Other Words
soul spirit, inner self
a phenomenon of something that happens with

7. Interpret

In your own words, describe why this superstition is false.

Possible response:

People used to think

that insects inside of

trees were gods. That is

not true, so knocking on

a tree or wood for good

luck will not work.

SUPERSTITION 5
Knocking on wood keeps misfortune away.

Where It Came From People used to believe that gods lived inside trees. If you knocked on wood when you wanted a favor, the tree gods would help you.

What's the Truth? In the past, people may have **mistaken** tree-dwelling insects for gods, says Linda Butler, **an entomologist** at West Virginia University. "Lots of noisy insects live inside trees," she says. "For instance, the larva of the pine sawyer beetle makes a loud gnawing sound when it chews on wood." ❖

The pine sawyer beetle got its name from the sawing noise the larva makes as it chews the wood.

Key Vocabulary
> **misfortune** *n.*, bad luck
> **mistaken** *v.*, mixed up, confused

In Other Words
an entomologist a person who studies insects

Selection Review Superstitions: The Truth Uncovered

A. Complete the chart below. Explain why people believed each superstition, and the truth about each.

Superstition	Why People Believed It	The Truth
Ravens predict death.	People saw ravens in places associated with dying.	Tame ravens are very friendly.
Walking under a ladder is bad luck.	Walking through a triangle could let evil out.	Triangles do not make ladders unsafe.
Throwing salt wards off evil.	People threw salt into the eyes of spirits who were going to steal it.	There are no salt-stealing spirits.

B. Answer the questions.

1. How do the nonfiction text features help you understand what the magazine article is about?

The headings describe each superstition; the pictures show the truth behind each.

2. What do superstitions cause people to do? Give one example from the text and what it caused people to believe.

Possible response: Superstitions cause people to act in ways that don't make sense. Noisy insects live inside trees. People thought they were gods and knocked on the trees for good luck.

Reflect and Assess

WRITING: Write About Literature

A. Plan your writing. Read the opinion below. Decide if you agree or disagree with it. List examples from each text to support it. *Answers will vary.*

Opinion: People make up superstitions when they want to feel in control of something they don't understand.

The Experiment	Superstitions: The Truth Uncovered

B. What is your opinion? Write an opinion statement. Remember to use examples from both texts and your own experience to support your opinion.

Students should support their answers with examples from the selections and their own experiences.

_____

_____

_____

_____

_____

_____

_____

_____

Integrate the Language Arts

LITERARY ANALYSIS: Analyze Plot: Climax

A good story has a plot that keeps you guessing. Stories often start when a character has a **problem**. The **rising action** is the events that lead up to the **climax**, which is the most exciting part. The **falling action** is the events that follow the climax, and any leftover problems are solved during the **resolution**.

A. The plot diagram below contains elements of the plot of "The Experiment." Complete the diagram by filling in the missing events, the climax, and the resolution.

Plot Diagram

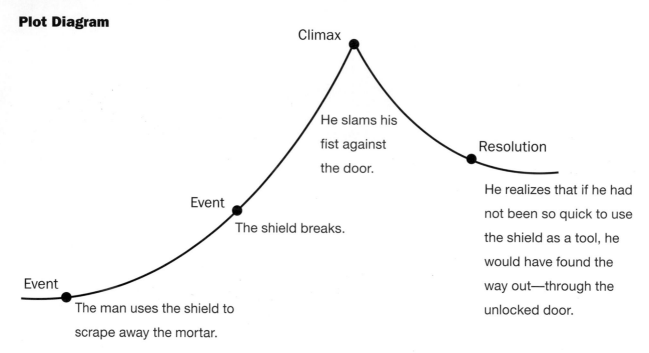

Climax

He slams his fist against the door.

Resolution

He realizes that if he had not been so quick to use the shield as a tool, he would have found the way out—through the unlocked door.

Event

The shield breaks.

Event

The man uses the shield to scrape away the mortar.

B. Brainstorm two alternate climaxes and two alternate resolutions. *Answers will vary.*

Climax:

1. _____

2. _____

Resolution:

1. _____

2. _____

C. Choose one climax and resolution. Write a paragraph that tells the new ending to the story. *Answers will vary.*

Just then, the man saw _____

_____

_____.

VOCABULARY STUDY: Prefixes

A **prefix** is a word part added at the beginning of a word in order to change the word's meaning. *Answers will vary. Possible responses are shown.*

A. *Dis-* is a common prefix that means "not" or "the opposite of." Write what you think each word means. Use a resource to check if you are not sure. Then write a sentence using the word.

Word	What It Means	Sentence
disability	to not be able to do something	A person with a disability might not be able to walk.
disagree	to not agree	My brother and I disagree about which baseball team should win the game.
disband	to fall apart	My favorite music group disbanded because the drummer left.
discourage	to not feel hopeful	I feel discouraged when I do not succeed at something I enjoy.
disengage	to undo or not start	The security guard disengaged the security lock of the prison to let in the visitors.

B. What are other words you know that contain the prefix *dis-*? List them in the chart below. Write the definition of each word. Use a dictionary to confirm the meanings.

Word	Definition
discolor	to change the color
discomfort	unease, the feeling of not being comfortable
discontinue	to not continue
dislike	to not enjoy

C. Use the chart above to write a sentence for each word you listed.

1. My white shirts are discolored because I washed them with red clothes.

2. I feel discomfort when I have to go to the dentist and have my cavities filled.

3. My favorite brand of chips are discontinued.

4. I dislike bitter foods because they do not taste good.

Prepare to Read

▶ **Building Bridges**
▶ **The Right Words at the Right Time**

Key Vocabulary

A. How well do you know these words? Circle a rating for each word. Check your understanding of each word by circling *yes* or *no.* Then, write a definition in your own words. If you are unsure of a word's meaning, refer to the Vocabulary Glossary, page 764, in your student text.

Rating Scale	
1	I have never seen this word before.
2	I am not sure of the word's meaning.
3	I know this word and can teach the word's meaning to someone else.

Key Word	Check Your Understanding	Deepen Your Understanding
❶ **career** (ku-**rear**) *noun* **Rating:** 1 2 3	Usually, a **career** in medicine requires a college degree and many years of job training. **(Yes)** No	My definition: *Answers will vary.*
❷ **comedian** (ku-**mē**-dē-un) *noun* **Rating:** 1 2 3	A **comedian** has the ability to make people laugh. **(Yes)** No	My definition: *Answers will vary.*
❸ **consent** (kun-**sent**) *noun* **Rating:** 1 2 3	It is best to have a friend's **consent** before borrowing his bicycle. **(Yes)** No	My definition: *Answers will vary.*
❹ **engineer** (en-ju-**near**) *noun* **Rating:** 1 2 3	An **engineer** needs an education to plan difficult projects. Yes **(No)**	My definition: *Answers will vary.*

Key Word	Check Your Understanding	Deepen Your Understanding
5 obstacle (**ob**-sti-kul) *noun* **Rating:** 1 2 3	A strong person gives up when there is an **obstacle** in the way. Yes (No)	My definition: *Answers will vary.* _____ _____ _____ .
6 project (**prah**-jekt) *noun* **Rating:** 1 2 3	Starting a **project** can be hard, but completing it is rewarding. (Yes) No	My definition: *Answers will vary.* _____ _____ _____ .
7 react (rē-**akt**) *verb* **Rating:** 1 2 3	Most people **react** calmly in a car accident. Yes (No)	My definition: *Answers will vary.* _____ _____ _____ .
8 stubborn (**stu**-burn) *adjective* **Rating:** 1 2 3	A person is **stubborn** by not admitting he or she is wrong. (Yes) No	My definition: *Answers will vary.* _____ _____ _____ .

B. Use one of the Key Vocabulary words to describe a goal in your life. What might keep you from reaching it?

Answers will vary.

_____

Before Reading Building Bridges

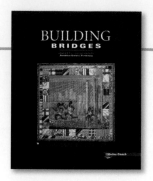

LITERARY ANALYSIS: Character

Authors show what a character is like with **description** and **dialogue.**

A. Read the passage. In the chart below, write how description and dialogue show what Mama Lil is like.

> ### Look Into the Text
>
> Mama Lil and I had been butting heads ever since I could remember. And the older I got, the more at odds we were.
>
> She thought I weighed too much and dressed badly. I thought she smoked too much and overdid it with her fake gold chains. Time after time, she'd asked me, "How you ever gonna land a decent man with them chunky arms and those T-shirts that put your navel on parade? No self-respecting seventeen-year-old should be letting it all hang out like *that*."

Mama Lil	
Description: She smokes too much. She wears too many fake gold chains.	Dialogue: "How you ever going to land a decent man?"

B. Answer the question about Mama Lil.

What do description and dialogue tell you about Mama Lil? _Possible response:_ Mama Lil has old-fashioned values and does not take care of herself. She wears too much jewelry.

READING STRATEGY: Clarify Ideas

HOW TO CLARIFY IDEAS

1. **Reread** When you don't understand a part, ask a question. Then reread to answer it.

2. **Read On** Keep reading to clarify what you don't understand.

A. Read the passage. Use the strategies above to clarify the ideas as you read. Answer the questions below.

Look Into the Text

Truth be told, Mama Lil was scared of something she didn't know. She hardly ever left our neighborhood in Brooklyn. To her, the Brooklyn Bridge was a mystery.

And I think that deep down Mama Lil was afraid something bad would happen to me, the same way it happened to my mama and daddy. Also, Mama Lil couldn't read or write very well. I read most of her mail to her and helped her sign her checks.

1. What does Bebe mean when she says Mama Lil was "scared of something she didn't know"?

   Mama Lil is not comfortable with unfamiliar things.

2. How is Mama Lil and Bebe's relationship different from a typical adult and child's relationship?

   Mama Lil and Bebe take care of each other. Mama Lil needs Bebe to read and write for her.

B. Write the strategy you used to answer each question.

   Number 1: Read On.

   Number 2: Reread.

Selection Review Building Bridges

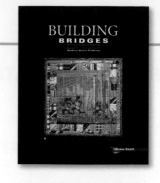

 What Influences How You Act?
Find out how people get to where they want to go.

A. In "Building Bridges," Bebe has a goal. The way she acts toward Mama Lil determines the story's outcome. Complete the map below.

Goal-and-Outcome Map

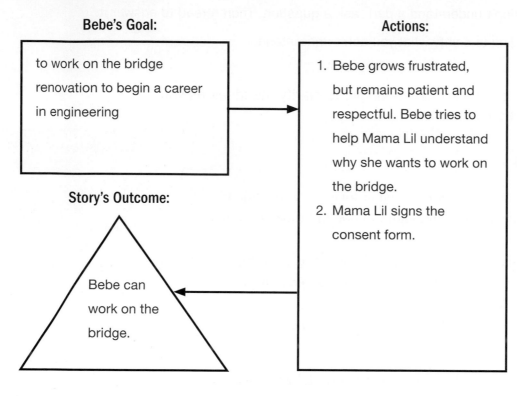

Bebe's Goal:

to work on the bridge renovation to begin a career in engineering

Actions:

1. Bebe grows frustrated, but remains patient and respectful. Bebe tries to help Mama Lil understand why she wants to work on the bridge.
2. Mama Lil signs the consent form.

Story's Outcome:

Bebe can work on the bridge.

B. Use what you know about the characters to answer the questions.

1. Why does Mama Lil not want Bebe to work on the bridge renovation?

Mama Lil is afraid because she doesn't want to lose Bebe. She wants Bebe to stay in the neighborhood and to work at a job she knows something about.

2. How does Bebe react to Mama Lil? Use **react** in your answer.

Possible response: Bebe reacts patiently, but she is clearly frustrated. Bebe does not back down, because she wants to work on the bridge. She helps Mama Lil understand the consent form.

3. How might Bebe's relationship with Mama Lil change after this incident?

Possible response: Mama Lil will trust that Bebe will not leave her. Bebe will feel that Mama Lil finally sees her for who she really is.

Connect Across Text
In "Building Bridges," Bebe knows what she wants in life. Read this memoir about what causes a teen to change his life.

THE RIGHT
WORDS
AT THE RIGHT TIME

by John Leguizamo

I was a nerd in junior high. A really bad nerd. I was seriously out of touch, especially the way I dressed...

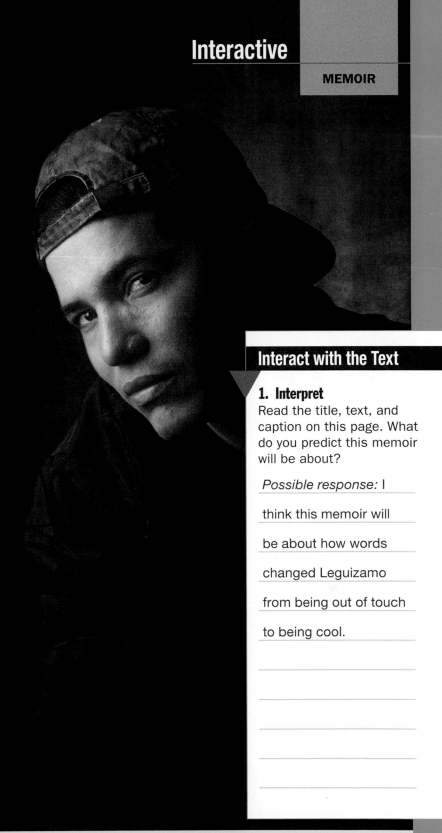

Interact with the Text

1. Interpret
Read the title, text, and caption on this page. What do you predict this memoir will be about?

Possible response: I think this memoir will be about how words changed Leguizamo from being out of touch to being cool.

Key Vocabulary
comedian *n.*, a person who makes people laugh

▲ John Leguizamo's family moved from Colombia to the United States when he was four. He grew up to become an award-winning actor, **comedian**, producer, and writer.

2. Clarify Ideas

Remember that breaking up a sentence when you read will help you find the main idea. Underline the sentence that illustrates the author's realization about his looks. In your own words, explain the main idea of the sentence.

Possible response:

Dressing badly will not

attract girls.

3. Memoir

Highlight words and phrases that show what the author was like when he was growing up. How do you know he is not like that anymore? Explain.

Possible response: He is

famous and could not be

successful if he stayed

the same. He also talks

about the past.

When you're a poor kid at a poor school, you worry a lot about how you look all the time, how much money you're spending on clothes and all that. I had problems, man. I wore **high waters**. And my shoes? Forget about it. I had fake sneakers—you know, the kind your mother finds in those big wire bins.

"Hey, John, here's one I like! Go find the one that matches!"

"I found it, Ma, but it's only a three and a half."

"Don't worry. We'll cut out the toes."

So there I am, pants too high, sneakers too tight, underwear without leg holes. I was the **Quasimodo of Jackson Heights**. Then it hits me: this is no way to get girls. So I had my mission then: become cool.

I totally changed. I hung out with the gangsters. Cut class. By the time I got to high school, I was getting in trouble all the time.

What I loved most was **cracking** jokes in school. I liked keeping the kids laughing. Even the teachers laughed sometimes, which was the best part. See, I was still so **out of it** in a way—too cool to hang with

Leguizamo has become a successful comedian and actor. He has been nominated for two Tony Awards for work in theater. He won an Emmy Award in 1999 for work in television.

In Other Words

high waters pants that were too short
Quasimodo of Jackson Heights strange-looking one in my neighborhood. Quasimodo is a deformed man in *The Hunchback of Notre Dame*, a book by Victor Hugo.

cracking telling
out of it odd, different from everyone else

the nerds, not cool enough to be with the *real* cool guys—I figured my only value was to be funny. I enjoyed people enjoying me.

Anyway, one day during my junior year, I was walking down the hallway, making jokes as usual, when Mr. Zufa, my math teacher, pulled me aside. I got collared by the teachers all the time, so I didn't think much about it. Mr. Zufa looked at me and started talking.

"Listen," he says, "instead of being so **obnoxious** all the time—instead of wasting all that energy in class—why don't you rechannel your hostility and humor into something productive? Have you ever thought about being a comedian?"

I didn't talk back to Mr. Zufa like I usually would have. I was quiet. I probably said something like, "Yeah, cool, man," but for the rest of the day, I couldn't get what he said out of my head.

It started to hit me, like, "Wow, I'm going to be a loser all my life." And I really didn't want to be a loser. I wanted to be somebody.

But that one moment Mr. Zufa collared me was the turning point in my life. Everything kind of **converged**, you know? The planets aligned.

But the big change didn't happen overnight.

Eventually, I got into New York University, where I did student films. One of the movies won **a Spielberg Focus Award**, and suddenly my life changed.

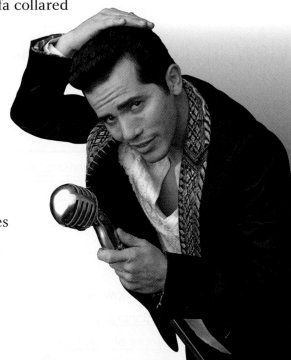

In Other Words
obnoxious annoying
converged came together, worked out
a Spielberg Focus Award an award given by Steven Spielberg, a famous movie director

4. Interpret
What happened as a result of Mr. Zufa's lecture?

Leguizamo realized that unless he made changes, he would be a loser all his life.

5. Memoir
Leguizamo explains that he did not immediately change from "a loser" into "somebody." What do you think were some of the steps he took in order to change?

Possible response: He probably took acting classes so he could learn from experts. He may have started paying attention to his behavior.

6. Interpret

Leguizamo is now an adult, recalling his days in school. In your own words, explain why he is still so grateful to Mr. Zufa.

Possible response:

Leguizamo is grateful

that Mr. Zufa took

the time to notice his

talents, even though he

was difficult in class.

I got an agent and wound up as a guest villain on *Miami Vice*. That started my **career**.

I've run into Mr. Zufa a bunch of times since high school and told him how his advice turned my life around. And I'm not just saying that. Here's a guy who was able to look beneath all the stuff I pulled in class and find some kind of merit in it, something worth pursuing. How cool is that? ❖

In Other Words
minor person under the age of 18
intervene get involved to prevent or solve problems

Selection Review The Right Words at the Right Time

A. Underline the main part of the sentence below. Then circle the parts of the sentence that support it. Use the punctuation to help you see the parts.

> Anyway, one day during my junior year, I was walking down the hallway, making jokes as usual, when Mr. Zufa, my math teacher, pulled me aside.

B. Answer the questions.

1. How is this memoir similar to a story? How is it different?

It is similar because the memoir has a beginning, a middle, and an end. It is different because a memoir is nonfiction. It is a personal account of a person's life.

2. Is there an adult who has had a positive impact on your life? How has this person influenced your decisions? Write your ideas in a brief paragraph.

Answers will vary.

Reflect and Assess

WRITING: Write About Literature

A. Plan your writing. List examples of how Bebe and Leguizamo make choices. *Answers will vary.*

Bebe	John Leguizamo

B. What have you learned about making choices by reading about Bebe and Leguizamo? Write a journal entry describing what you've learned. Give examples from both texts.

Students should support their answers with examples from the selections.

_____

_____

_____

_____

_____

_____

_____

_____

_____

Integrate the Language Arts

▶ **Building Bridges**
▶ **The Right Words at the Right Time**

LITERARY ANALYSIS: Dialect

Dialect is a version of language used by a specific group or used in a specific region. Dialect can include special expressions and pronunciations.

Answers will vary. Possible responses are shown.

A. List three examples of dialect from "Building Bridges." Use context clues to explain what each example means.

Example of Dialect	Meaning
"That grit-work ain't no place for you."	"Hard work like that is not for you."
"'Ain't no black woman doing no engine-ing,' she'd said."	"I've never seen a black woman who became an engineer."
"'What little bit of dreaming I got left in me,' she said, 'I'm putting to you.'"	"Your dreams are my dreams."

B. Describe how the use of dialect helped you better understand each character in "Building Bridges."

The use of dialect helped me better visualize the setting, and it helped me know more about Bebe. I was able to use what the characters said in order to find out what they are like.

C. List examples of dialect from "The Right Words at the Right Time.""

"I wore highwaters.", "I was still so out of it in a way.", "Yeah, cool, man."

VOCABULARY STUDY: Prefixes

A **prefix** is a word part that is added to the beginning of a word. It changes the word's meaning. *Answers will vary. Possible responses are shown.*

A. *Pre-* is a common prefix that means before. Write what you think each word means. Confirm the definition for each word in the dictionary.

Word	Meaning
precaution	something you do in advance to avoid danger
predict	to say what will happen before it occurs
prepay	to pay for something before you buy it
prevent	to stop something from happening before it occurs
preview	to look at or see something before anyone else

B. The chart below shows some common prefixes and their meanings. Complete the chart by listing words that contain each prefix.

Prefix	Meaning	Words
dis-	not, opposite of	disappear
non-	not	nonsense
re-	back or again	rewrite
sub-	below, less than, under	subway
un-	not	unfold

C. Write a definition for each of these words.

reconsider ___to consider again_____

unsatisfactory ___not satisfactory_____

dishonest ___not honest_____

nonstop ___something that does not stop_____

subconscious ___something that is under or beneath consciousness_____

Prepare to Read

▶ **The Open Window**
▶ **One in a Million**

Key Vocabulary

A. How well do you know these words? Circle a rating for each word. Check your understanding of each word by choosing the correct synonym. Then complete the sentences. If you are unsure of a word's meaning, refer to the Vocabulary Glossary, page 764, in your student text.

Rating Scale

1	I have never seen this word before.
2	I am not sure of the word's meaning.
3	I know this word and can teach the word's meaning to someone else.

Key Word	Check Your Understanding	Deepen Your Understanding
1 confident (**kon**-fu-dunt) *adjective* Rating: 1 2 3	To be **confident** is to be _____. careful (certain)	A time I was confident was when _____ *Possible response:* I took a test I studied very hard for _____ _____ _____.
2 convince (kun-**vins**) *verb* Rating: 1 2 3	To **convince** is to _____. (persuade) lie	Advertisements convince people that _____ *Possible response:* their lives would improve if they bought that item _____ _____ _____.
3 doubt (dowt) *verb* Rating: 1 2 3	If you **doubt** something, you _____ it. believe (question)	When I doubt what a friend tells me, I respond by _____ *Possible response:* asking more questions or asking for proof _____ _____ _____.
4 foolish (**fü**-lish) *adjective* Rating: 1 2 3	To be **foolish** is to be _____. serious (unwise)	People are foolish when _____ *Possible response:* they spend more money than they make _____ _____ _____.

30   **Unit 1:** Think Again

Key Word	Check Your Understanding	Deepen Your Understanding
5 **nerves** (**nurvz**) *noun* **Rating:** 1 2 3	To suffer from **nerves** is to experience _____. (**anxiety**) **pride**	To get rid of an attack of nerves, I can _____ *Possible response:* breathe deeply and close my eyes _____ _____ .
6 **shock** (**shok**) *noun* **Rating:** 1 2 3	To experience **shock** is to be filled with extreme _____. **enthusiasm** (**surprise**)	I would be in shock if *Possible response:* it snowed in July _____ _____ _____ .
7 **tragedy** (**tra**-ju-dē) *noun* **Rating:** 1 2 3	A **tragedy** is a type of _____. **celebration** (**misfortune**)	Someone I know experienced a tragedy when _____ *Possible response:* his house burned down _____ _____ _____ .
8 **worthless** (**wurth**-lus) *adjective* **Rating:** 1 2 3	Something that is **worthless** is _____. (**useless**) **interesting**	An example of an object that I have that is worthless is *Possible response:* a broken CD player _____ _____ _____ .

B. Use one of the Key Vocabulary words to write about a time someone influenced your behavior.

Answers will vary. _____

_____

Before Reading The Open Window

LITERARY ANALYSIS: Character and Plot

You can learn what a character is like from **dialogue** and a character's **actions.** Their actions create the plot.

A. Read the passage below. Pay attention to dialogue and to Framton's actions, or the plot. In the chart, write what the dialogue tells you about Framton.

Look Into the Text

> Framton Nuttel tried to think of something to talk about with the girl. He also wondered what he would say to the aunt. At his sister's recommendation, he had come to their home in the country to rest and cure his nerves. But he doubted whether this visit with total strangers was going to help him.
> "I know how it will be," his sister had said before he left for the country. "You won't speak to anyone down there. Your nerves will be worse than ever from moping."

Framton's Actions	What the Dialogue Says	What Is Framton Like?
Framton goes to the country to rest his nerves.	Framton's sister says he won't talk to anyone. He will mope and make his nerves worse.	Framton is someone who gets nervous very easily and is uncomfortable around others.

B. Answer the question about the plot.

Will Framton's visit to the country be restful? Why or why not?   His visit will not be restful. Framton is a nervous person. He probably will not talk to anyone or have a good time.

READING STRATEGY: Clarify Vocabulary

How to Clarify Vocabulary

1. **Find Context Clues** Look for clue words near the unfamiliar word.

2. **Analyze the Clues** Combine the clues with what you know to figure out the meaning of the unfamiliar word.

3. **Replace** Use the meaning in the sentence. Check that it makes sense.

A. Read the passage. Use the strategies above to clarify vocabulary. Answer the questions below. *Answers will vary.*

Look Into the Text

"On this day three years ago, her husband, her two young brothers, and their little brown dog left through that window to go hunting. They never came back. On the way to their favorite hunting spot, they all drowned. It had been a very wet summer. Places that used to be safe to walk across were not safe. The marsh gave way suddenly without warning. Their bodies were never recovered. That was the dreadful part of it."

1. What word don't you know? _____

2. What words and phrases give you clues to the word's meaning?_____

   _____

3. What do you already know about these words and phrases? _____

   _____

4. What is the meaning of the word?_____

B. Rewrite the sentence by replacing the original word with the meaning.

_____

_____

Does it make sense? Circle *yes* or *no*.   **Yes**   **No**

Selection Review The Open Window

 What Influences How You Act?
Find out how easily people can be fooled.

A. In "The Open Window," you found out how easy it was for Vera to influence Framton to run away. Complete the chart with Framton's and Vera's words and actions.

Characters	Words	Actions
Framton	says he doesn't know anyone from the country	listens to Vera's story
		thinks he sees ghosts
	needs complete rest for his nerves	runs from the house
Vera	invents a tragic story	acts confident
	tells Mrs. Sappleton that Framton is scared of dogs	scares Framton and makes him look foolish and strange

B. Use the information in the chart to answer the questions about the characters and the plot.

1. Why is Framton an easy person to shock and influence?

Framton is easy to shock because he is nervous and easily excited. Also, he has never met Vera before so he doesn't know what she's like.

2. How might the story have been different if Vera had been less confident? Use **confident** in your answer.

Possible response: If Vera had been less confident, she might not have tried to influence Framton by telling him a tragic story.

3. Why do you think Vera chooses to treat Framton this way?

Possible response: Vera senses Framton is nervous and easy to shock. She may want to expose his weakness.

Interactive
One in a Million

a traditional Middle Eastern tale

Connect Across Texts

In "The Open Window," the girl **convinces** *Framton of something. What is Hodja convinced of in this folk tale?*

Nasruddin Hodja looked at his donkey and frowned. The beast was **a bag of bones** and had a dirty, shaggy coat. It stood under a tree, **dully chewing a clump of grass**. "Look at you," Hodja sneered. "You are completely **worthless** to me. All you do is stand under that tree. You refuse every order I give you!"

The lazy donkey didn't even look at Hodja. It kept **chomping away**.

"That's it!" Hodja cried in frustration. "I'm going to sell you!"

So the next day Hodja led the scrawny creature to the crowded marketplace in the center of the village. He was grateful for the thirty **dinars** a **foolish** man offered him for the beast. Hodja went on with his business as the buyer led the hopeless creature away.

Later, as Hodja wound his way out of the marketplace, he noticed a crowd of eager shoppers. Curious to see what treasure they were after, Hodja pushed through to the center of the group. He was startled to see his donkey! The beast's new owner was shouting, "Look at this fine animal! Have you ever seen a better donkey? See how clean and strong it is! You will never find a better worker. Who will bid for this exceptional creature?"

The buyers pressed forward eagerly. "What a prize! What a find!" they murmured excitedly. One shopper offered forty dinars for the donkey.

Key Vocabulary
- **convince** *v.*, to make someone believe something
- **worthless** *adj.*, useless
- **foolish** *adj.*, not wise, silly

In Other Words
a bag of bones very thin
dully chewing a clump of grass chewing some grass in a slow, bored way
chomping away eating, chewing
dinars gold coins

Interact with the Text

1. Folk Tale
The setting of a folk tale reflects the culture it comes from. Underline words that tell you about the setting. Write a sentence describing where Hodja lives.

Hodja lives in a small village and visits the market to buy and sell things.

2. Clarify Vocabulary
Circle the clues that help you figure out what *sneered* means. Rewrite the sentence, replacing *sneered* with the meaning.

Possible response:

"Look at you," Hodja said with a disgusted expression

3. Interpret
How might he have acted differently if the new owner did not praise the donkey? Why?

Possible response: Hodja

probably would not have

bought back his donkey

for more than it was

worth because he would

not have doubted his

original opinion.

Another man offered fifty. A third offered fifty-five!

Puzzlement furrowed Hodja's brow. "I thought that donkey was just an ordinary animal," he said to himself, scratching his scraggly beard. "Was I a fool? It is obviously very special. It's one in a million . . ."

The new owner swept his arm toward the donkey and cried, "How can you **pass up** the chance to own such a magnificent beast? See how the muscles ripple under the smooth, silky coat. Look at those bright, intelligent eyes . . ."

Hodja squeezed his way to the front of the crowd. The man's **flowery words** floated through the warm air, filling Hodja's ears. "Seventy-five dinars once," the man yelled. "Seventy-five dinars twice . . ."

Hodja's skin tingled. He raised his hand excitedly and shouted, "I bid eighty dinars!" ❖

In Other Words
Puzzlement furrowed Hodja's brow. Hodja looked confused.
pass up miss, not take
flowery words nice words, nice description

Cultural Background
Nasruddin Hodja is a popular character in Middle Eastern tales. Sometimes he is a fool, but sometimes he is wise. He is known by different names throughout the Middle East.

Selection Review One in a Million

A. Below is one word from "One in a Million." Write two clues from the selection that help you understand the word's meaning. Then write what the word means.

Word	First Clue	Second Clue	Word Meaning
scrawny	bag of bones	dirty, shaggy coat	*Possible response:* skinny and ugly

B. Answer the questions.

1. How did knowing you were reading a folk tale help you to clarify the vocabulary?

Possible response: I knew that I should look for words and phrases that show details about the

culture the folk tale came from.

2. Imagine you are the seller of Hodja's donkey. Describe it to a buyer. Reread the text to find ideas.

Possible response: This donkey is the best donkey I have ever seen! He is one in a million! Watch

how quickly he eats his lunch!

Reflect and Assess

WRITING: Write About Literature

A. Plan your writing. Read the opposing opinions. Put an *X* next to the opinion you agree with. Then list three examples from each text to support it. *Answers will vary.*

☐ **Opinion 1:** The characters in these stories were tricked because they were foolish.

☐ **Opinion 2:** The characters in these stories were tricked because they met confident, talented liars.

The Open Window	One in a Million

B. What is your opinion? Write an opinion statement. Remember to use the text evidence you listed in the chart to support your statement.

Students should support their answers with examples from the selections.

_____

_____

_____

_____

_____

_____

_____

_____

Integrate the Language Arts

LITERARY ANALYSIS: Compare Settings

The **setting** is where and when a story takes place. Authors can tell the setting directly or they can suggest the setting and let you imagine it. *Possible responses are shown.*

A. List details about the settings of both selections.

The Open Window	One in a Million
Framton is at a house in the country.	There is a tree that the donkey always stands under.
The room in Mrs. Sappleton's house makes Framton think she is married.	The majority of the story takes place in a village.
The time of year is October.	There is a crowded marketplace in the middle of the village.
It is a warm day. Outside it is muddy.	

B. Answer the questions.

1. Compare the way each author describes the setting.

The author of "The Open Window" tells details about the setting. The author of "One in a Million" leaves the setting to the reader's imagination.

2. What picture did you form in your mind of the setting of "One in a Million"?

A crowded marketplace in the center of the village.

3. How does the setting of "The Open Window" affect the characters?

The niece tells tales because she is bored living in the country. The setting affects Framton because he goes to the country to calm his nerves, but instead his visit scares him.

C. Imagine that "The Open Window" takes place in a big city. Describe how the characters and plot of the story might be different.

The niece might not be as bored. She would not have told Framton that lie, but she might have told him another lie. She might have done something else like give Framton the wrong directions in the city.

VOCABULARY STUDY: Suffixes

A **suffix** is a word part added to the end of a word. A suffix changes a word's meaning. *Answers will vary. Possible responses are shown.*

A. *–Ful* is a common suffix that means "full of." Write what you think each word means. Confirm the definition of each word in the dictionary.

Word	Meaning
careful	with care
harmful	with harm
mindful	with presence of mind, thoughtful
thoughtful	with thought
useful	able to use

B. The chart below shows some common suffixes and their meanings. Complete the chart by listing words you've heard that contain each suffix.

Suffix	Meaning	Words
-logy	the study of	biology
-ly	like	slowly
-ment	result	pavement
-ness	the state of	emptiness
-ous	possessing the quality of	joyous

C. Write a definition for each of these words.

clearly ___in a way that is easy to understand___

judgment ___the result of judging something___

weakness ___the state of being weak___

zoology ___the study of animals___

tremulous ___affected by trembling___

Key Vocabulary Review

A. Read each sentence. Circle the word that best fits into each sentence.

1. A person might change his or her (**career**/ **superstition**) several times.

2. It is important to get someone's (**evidence** / **consent**) if you want to borrow something.

3. People usually (**react** / **escape**) to a joke by laughing.

4. You might feel (**stubborn** / **confident**) if someone compliments you.

5. A (**worthless** / **foolish**) person might think school is unimportant.

6. A deadly house fire is a (**tragedy** / **failure**).

7. Most people have to overcome an (**experiment** / **obstacle**) to reach their goals.

8. A (**project** / **belief**) requires hard work and preparation.

B. Use your own words to write what each Key Vocabulary word means. Then write a synonym for each word. *Answers will vary. Possible responses are shown.*

Key Word	My Definition	Synonym
1. belief	something you think is true	opinion
2. comedian	someone who makes people laugh	comic
3. convince	to persuade someone	win over
4. doubt	to not believe someone or something	question
5. experiment	a test to learn something	trial
6. misfortune	something bad you do not expect	bad luck
7. mistaken	confused	mixed up
8. shock	a surprise or sudden blow	surprise

belief	• consent	escape	foolish	obstacle	stubborn
career	• convince	• evidence	misfortune	• project	superstition
comedian	doubt	experiment	mistaken	• react	tragedy
confident	engineer	failure	nerves	shock	worthless

• **Academic Vocabulary**

C. Complete the sentences. *Answers will vary. Possible responses are shown.*

1. An **engineer** is someone who <u>plans or designs buildings</u>

2. I suffer from **nerves** when <u>I speak in front of a large group of people</u>

3. A person might try to **escape** if <u>he or she is in danger or frightened</u>

4. A detective might study **evidence** to determine <u>who committed a crime and how it happened</u>

5. I know a person who is **stubborn** about <u>his views on politics</u>

6. One **superstition** people might believe in is <u>the number 13 is bad luck</u>

7. A pair of glasses with no lenses is **worthless** because <u>they will not help you see</u>

8. I experienced a **failure** when <u>we lost the big game</u>

Prepare to Read

▸ Genes: All in the Family
▸ How to See DNA

Key Vocabulary

A. How well do you know these words? Circle a rating for each word. Check your understanding of each word by circling *yes* or *no*. Then, complete the sentences. If you are unsure of a word's meaning, refer to the Vocabulary Glossary, page 764, in your student text.

Rating Scale

1 I have never seen this word before.

2 I am not sure of the word's meaning.

3 I know this word and can teach the word's meaning to someone else.

Key Word	Check Your Understanding	Deepen Your Understanding
❶ control (kun-**trōl**) *verb* **Rating:** 1 2 3	People can **control** how tall they will be. Yes (No)	One thing I control in my life is _Possible response:_ how much I study
❷ extraction (ik-**strak**-shun) *noun* **Rating:** 1 2 3	A doctor can perform an **extraction** of a rusty nail from a patient's foot. (Yes) No	After a tooth extraction, people usually _____ *Possible response:* cannot eat for a few hours
❸ inherit (in-**hair**-ut) *verb* **Rating:** 1 2 3	If you **inherit** a ring, you buy it with your own money. Yes (No)	Something I would like to inherit is _Possible response:_ a photograph of my grandmother as a child
❹ molecule (**mo**-li-kyūl) *noun* **Rating:** 1 2 3	A **molecule** of water is much larger than a school bus. Yes (No)	When scientists look at molecules, they need special equipment, such as _Possible response:_ a powerful microscope

Key Word	Check Your Understanding	Deepen Your Understanding
5 **sequence** (sē-kwuns) *noun* **Rating:** 1 2 3	The **sequence** of the alphabet is *d, t, u, c, r, l.* Yes (**No**)	The sequence of events in my morning routine is _____ *Possible response:* I get up, eat breakfast, and get dressed _____ _____.
6 **trait** (trāt) *noun* **Rating:** 1 2 3	A physical **trait**, such as hair or eye color, comes from a person's biological parents. (**Yes**) No	The trait I have that I like best is *Possible response:* my curly hair _____ _____ _____.
7 **transmit** (trans-**mit**) *verb* **Rating:** 1 2 3	When you cough on someone, you usually **transmit** germs. (**Yes**) No	One way to transmit a message without speaking is ____ *Possible response:* to write the message on a piece of paper _____ _____.
8 **unique** (yū-**nēk**) *adjective* **Rating:** 1 2 3	My sister's hair color is **unique** because it looks just like mine. Yes (**No**)	A unique thing about my friend is *Possible response:* the sound she makes when she laughs _____ _____.

B. Use one of the Key Vocabulary words to write about a physical characteristic you have. How do you feel about it?

Answers will vary. _____

_____

LITERARY ANALYSIS: Science Article

A **science article** is **expository nonfiction** that gives facts about the natural world. Key terms are words you should know about the topic. Heads and diagrams in a science article help explain the ideas.

A. Read the passage below. Identify the facts and key terms about genes. Write the facts and key terms in the Main-Idea Tree.

Look Into the Text

What Is a Gene?

The word *gene* has several meanings, but in essence, a gene is an instruction that tells your body how to work. The instruction is stored as a code in the molecule DNA.

Main-Idea Tree

What Is a Gene?

Fact: A gene tells the body how to work.

Fact: A gene is stored as code in the molecule DNA.

Key Term: *code*

Key Term: molecule DNA

B. Answer the question.

What do the facts and the key terms tell you about genes? Genes tell your body how to work. They have a specific code in your DNA.

READING STRATEGY: Self-Question

Reading Strategy
Ask Questions

HOW TO SELF-QUESTION

1. **Ask Questions** Pay attention to important ideas, text features, and diagrams.

2. **Write Your Questions** Write *Who, What, Where, When, Why,* and *How* questions.

3. **Answer the Questions** Use the text and visuals to help answer your questions.

A. Read the passage. Use the strategies above to self-question as you read. Complete the chart below.

Look Into the Text

Where Do My Genes Come From?

Your genes come from your parents, theirs come from their parents, and so on—all the way back to the first living thing that ever existed. Genes are passed down through families, and that's why you probably look a bit like your parents. Physical characteristics, like long eyelashes, red hair, freckles, or blue eyes, run in families because they are controlled by genes.

Type of Question	Ask Your Questions	Answer Your Questions
Where?	Where do your genes come from?	your parents
Why?	Why do you look like your parents?	Genes are passed down through families.
What?	What are some types of physical characteristics?	red hair, freckles, blue eyes
How?	How are physical characteristics controlled?	by genes

B. How did self-questioning help you understand the passage better?

Possible response: First, I looked for the facts that answered the *Where, Why, What,* and *How* questions. Then, I answered them.

Selection Review Genes: All in the Family

EQ How Do Families Affect Us?
Explore the science behind family resemblances.

A. In "Genes: All in the Family," you learned how scientific facts explain family resemblances. Complete the web below with facts from the article.

Idea Web

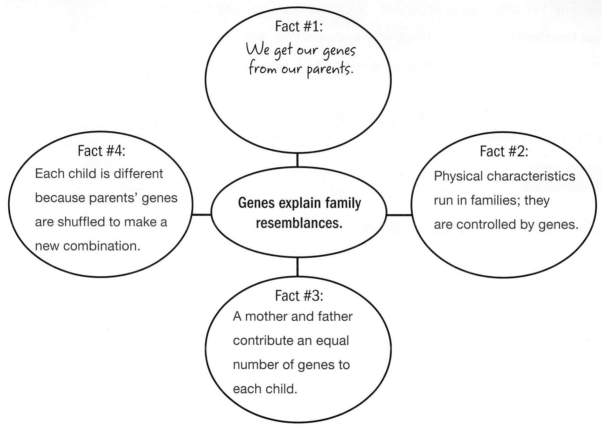

Fact #1:
We get our genes from our parents.

Fact #4:
Each child is different because parents' genes are shuffled to make a new combination.

Genes explain family resemblances.

Fact #2:
Physical characteristics run in families; they are controlled by genes.

Fact #3:
A mother and father contribute an equal number of genes to each child.

B. Use the information in the web to answer the questions.

1. Why do people often look similar to their parents?

Genes determine what we look like. Genes are passed down through families.

2. How is each child in a family unique? Use the word **unique** in your answer.

Possible response: Each child has a unique set of genes, so he or she has different characteristics.

3. Why is it important for scientists to study the relationship between genes and families?

Possible response: It is important for scientists to study genes because they can learn how different diseases run in families. This can help them find ways to cure people.

How to See **DNA** by the Genetic Science Learning Center

Connect Across Texts

You read about DNA in "Genes: All in the Family." In this science procedure, you will discover what DNA looks like.

The **traits** that you **inherit** from your parents are **determined** by DNA. This is true for all living things: The cells of every plant and animal contain DNA **molecules**. DNA carries the genetic information that determines what the plants and animals will look like, among other traits. You may wonder, though: What does DNA look like? Try this activity to find out.

How to See DNA

Purpose: In this activity, you will free DNA from the cells of green split peas. Then you will be able to see what DNA looks like.

You Will Need:

- 1/2 cup green split peas
- 1/8 teaspoon salt
- 1 cup cold water
- blender
- strainer
- measuring cups and spoons
- liquid detergent
- small glass tubes or containers
- meat tenderizer
- rubbing alcohol
- small wooden stir sticks

Key Vocabulary

trait *n.*, a certain way something is, a feature of something

inherit *v.*, to get things from family members who lived before us

molecule *n.*, a very small particle or piece of a substance

In Other Words

determined controlled

Interact with the Text

1. Self-Question
What questions do you have after reading the introduction to the science procedure? Write one of your questions.

Possible response: How can you extract DNA from a cell?

2. Science Procedure
Circle the sentence that tells you the goal of this science procedure. Write the goal in your own words.

Possible response: The goal is to find out what DNA looks like.

3. Interpret

Circle three words or phrases from Steps 1 and 2 that you might see in a recipe. How are recipes and science procedures similar?

Possible response:

Recipes and science

procedures both tell

you how to do or make

something by following

steps. They both have

lists of ingredients.

4. Self-Question

What question might the diagram *Pea Cell Structure* answer? Write a question and the answer.

Possible response:

Where is the pea's DNA

located? It is located in

the nucleus.

Step **1**

Blender Insanity!

Put the split peas, salt, and cold water in a blender. Put the blender lid in place. Blend on high for 15 seconds. The blender separates the pea cells from each other, so you now have a really thin pea-cell soup.

Step **2**

Soapy Peas

Pour the pea mixture through a strainer into a measuring cup. Add 2 tablespoons of liquid detergent to the strained peas. Swirl to mix.

Let the mixture sit for 5–10 minutes.

Why Do This?

Each pea cell is surrounded by a membrane, or outer covering. Inside the membrane is a nucleus. The nucleus is protected by another membrane. And inside the nucleus is the DNA.

To see the DNA, you have to break through both membranes. Detergent can handle this task.

A cell's membrane has lipid (fat) molecules with proteins connecting them. When detergent comes near the cell, it captures the lipids and proteins, breaking down the cell membrane and freeing the DNA from the nucleus.

Pea Cell Structure

membrane of nucleus

cell membrane

Step 3

Enzyme Power

<u>Pour</u> the mixture into the glass containers. <u>Fill</u> each container one-third full. Then, <u>add</u> a **pinch** of meat tenderizer (enzymes) to each container and <u>stir gently</u>. <u>Be careful!</u> If you stir too hard, you'll break up the DNA, making it harder to see.

Why Do This?
You may wonder why you are adding meat tenderizer to the soapy pea mixture.
X Meat tenderizer contains enzymes, proteins that help chemical reactions happen more quickly. Without enzymes, your body would **grind to a halt**.
    The DNA in the nucleus of a cell is protected by other kinds of proteins. Enzymes cut through those proteins.

Step 4

Alcohol Separation

Tilt your glass container. Slowly pour rubbing alcohol into the container and down the side. It should form a layer on top of the pea mixture. Continue pouring until you have about the same amount of alcohol as pea mixture in the container.

    DNA will rise from the layer of pea mixture into the alcohol layer. Use a wooden stick to draw the DNA from the alcohol. After you finish, you will have completed a DNA **extraction**!

Why Does This Happen?
Turn the page and find out...

Key Vocabulary
• **extraction** *n.*, the act of removing one thing from another thing

In Other Words
pinch little bit
grind to a halt stop suddenly and completely

7. Self-Question

Circle an interesting fact in the *Why Does This Happen?* box. Write a question you have about it.

Possible responses:

What other liquids are

less dense than water?

Could I use a liquid

other than alcohol in the

experiment?

Why Does This Happen?

Alcohol is **less dense than** water, so it floats on top. Because two separate layers are formed, all of the fats (lipids) and protein that you broke up in Steps 2 and 3, along with the DNA, have to decide: "Hmmm, which layer should I go to?"

Most particles and molecules will stay below the alcohol or dissolve in it. The DNA will float in the alcohol and will not be dissolved. This makes it easy to extract. ❖

In Other Words

less dense than not as thick as

Selection Review How to See DNA

A. Look at the question you wrote on page 47. Complete the sentences below.

1. The answer to my question is *Possible response:* meat tenderizer is used to extract the DNA

                                                                  .

2. I found the answer by *Possible response:* reading the steps carefully and looking at the visuals

     .

3. After learning this, I *Possible response:* am surprised that meat tenderizer could separate DNA from a pea

     .

B. Answer the questions.

1. Which features helped you understand this science procedure?

Possible response: The science procedure included a list of materials, clear photos, step-by-step directions, and an explanation of the purpose.

2. Was the science procedure easy to follow? Why or why not?

Possible response: It was easy to follow because there were clear photographs for each step.

Reflect and Assess

WRITING: Write About Literature

A. Plan your writing. Read the opposing opinions. Put an *X* next to the opinion you agree with. List examples from each selection to support your opinion. *Answers will vary.*

☐ **Opinion 1:** Genes are mainly responsible for determining who we are.

☐ **Opinion 2:** Genes are not the only thing responsible for determining who we are.

Genes: All in the Family	How to See DNA

B. What is your opinion? Write an opinion paragraph. Use the evidence you listed in the chart to support your opinion.

Students should support their answers with examples from the selections.

_____

_____

_____

_____

_____

_____

_____

_____

Integrate the Language Arts

LITERARY ANALYSIS: Analyze Author's Purpose

Authors decide which form of writing to use based on what information they want to tell their readers. Knowing an **author's purpose**, or reason for writing, helps you evaluate the information. Authors can write to inform, to persuade, to express feelings, or to describe. *Answers will vary. Possible responses are shown.*

A. List examples in the web from "Genes: All in the Family" that give you clues to the author's purpose for writing.

Idea Web

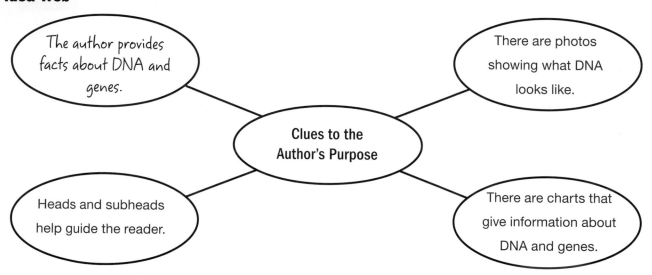

B. Answer the questions.

1. What is the author's purpose for writing? <u>The author wanted to inform readers about DNA.</u>

2. How does the author achieve his purpose? <u>He includes facts about DNA and genes. He also</u> <u>includes photos and diagrams to help the reader better understand a difficult topic.</u>

C. Answer the questions.

1. What form of writing might the author have chosen if he wanted to express his feelings about whether or not DNA is entirely responsible for who we are?
<u>The author might have chosen to write an essay or a short story because it would be based on opinion or</u> <u>feelings. The information might or might not be factual.</u>

2. How would this writing have achieved the author's purpose?
<u>The author would not have included photos, charts, headings, or facts.</u>

VOCABULARY STUDY: Context Clues

Context clues, or clues in a text, can help you figure out the meaning of an unfamiliar word. Two types of context clues include definitions and appositive definitions.

A. Read the text below. Circle the context clues that can help you figure out the meanings of the underlined words.

> Every person has a unique, (or one of a kind,) set of genes (except for identical twins). Genomes (are sets of genes.) There is a complete set of genes inside every cell in your body. To fit into this tiny space, the genes are packed up in an ingenious, (or clever, way.) Since you have two sets of genes, you have two options for everything. The option that (takes priority) is called the dominant gene.

B. Use the context clues that you circled, and write the meaning of each underlined word from the text above. Use a dictionary to check the definition.

Word	What It Means
dominant	more important or powerful
genomes	sets of genes
ingenious	clever
unique	one of a kind

C. Use the information in the chart to complete the sentences. *Possible responses are shown.*

1. If your mother's genes are **dominant**, you look like your mother.

2. Each set of **genomes** gives a person a mixture of their mother's and father's features.

3. The **ingenious** plan worked because it was so clever.

4. Every person is **unique** because we all have a different set of genes that makes our appearance and character different than anyone else's.

Prepare to Read

▶ Do Family Meals Matter?
▶ Fish Cheeks

Key Vocabulary

A. How well do you know these words? Circle a rating for each word. Check your understanding of each word by circling *yes* or *no*. Then, in your own words, write a definition for the word. If you are unsure of a word's meaning, refer to the Vocabulary Glossary, page 764, in your student text.

Rating Scale

1	I have never seen this word before.
2	I am not sure of the word's meaning.
3	I know this word and can teach the word's meaning to someone else.

Key Word	Check Your Understanding	Deepen Your Understanding
❶ appreciate (u-**prē**-shē-āt) *verb* **Rating:** 1 2 3	When you **appreciate** people, they usually become angry. Yes (No)	My definition: *Answers will vary.* _____.
❷ beneficial (be-nu-**fi**-shul) *adjective* **Rating:** 1 2 3	If something is **beneficial** you should throw it away immediately. Yes (No)	My definition: *Answers will vary.* _____.
❸ bond (**bond**) *noun* **Rating:** 1 2 3	Brothers can have a strong **bond**, even when they live in different cities. (Yes) No	My definition: *Answers will vary.* _____.
❹ consume (kun-**süm**) *verb* **Rating:** 1 2 3	Most cars **consume** gasoline. (Yes) No	My definition: *Answers will vary.* _____.

Key Word	Check Your Understanding	Deepen Your Understanding
5 data (**dā**-tu) *noun* Rating: 1 2 3	People who ask you to answer a set of questions could be collecting **data**. **(Yes)** No	My definition: _Answers will vary._ _____ _____ _____ _____ .
6 research (ri-**surch**) *noun* Rating: 1 2 3	Scientists use their **research** results to find new ways to cure illnesses. **(Yes)** No	My definition: _Answers will vary._ _____ _____ _____ _____ .
7 survey (**sur**-vā) *noun* Rating: 1 2 3	When you take a **survey**, you use a book to find the answers. Yes **(No)**	My definition: _Answers will vary._ _____ _____ _____ _____ .
8 united (yū-**nī**-tid) *adjective* Rating: 1 2 3	People who are **united** split into groups with opposite goals. Yes **(No)**	My definition: _Answers will vary._ _____ _____ _____ _____ .

B. Is spending time with your family important? Write a sentence using two of the Key Vocabulary words to tell what you think.

Answers will vary.
_____

Before Reading Do Family Meals Matter?

LITERARY ANALYSIS: Research Report

A **research report** presents factual information that a researcher has gathered about a topic.

A. Read the passage below. Find the facts about family meals. Restate the facts in the chart. Then, write what the data means.

Look Into the Text

Views on Family Meals

Is eating together really becoming less important to the American family? In a study called Project EAT (Eating Among Teens), 98% of the parents said that it was important to eat at least one meal together each day. Sixty-four percent of the adolescents in the study agreed with their parents.

Views	Facts or Data	What the Data Means
Parents	Ninety-eight percent of parents said it is important to eat at least one meal together each day.	Almost all the parents in the study want to eat with their families.
Teens	Sixty-four percent of the adolescents in the study agreed with their parents.	More than half of the teenagers in the study think they should eat with their parents at least once a day.

B. Compare the data. Complete the sentence about the research report.

The research report on family meals shows that   <u>nearly all parents and more than half of the teenagers</u>
   <u>surveyed think it is important to eat together.</u>

_____

_____

_____

READING STRATEGY: Find Question-Answer Relationships

Reading Strategy
Ask Questions

How to Find Question-Answer Relationships

1. **"Right There" Answers** You can often find answers right in the text.

2. **"Think and Search" Answers** Sometimes you need to put information together from different parts of the report to find an answer.

A. Read the passage. Use the strategies above to find question-answer relationships as you read. Answer the questions below.

Look Into the Text

> A survey for the National Center on Addiction and Substance Abuse found that:
> - 86% of teens who had dinner with their families five or more nights a week said they had never tried smoking, compared with 65% who had dinner with their families two nights a week or less
> - 68% of teens who had dinner with their families five nights a week or more reported never trying alcohol, compared to 47% of teens who ate dinner with their families two nights a week or less.
> - teens eating a family dinner five or more times a week were almost twice as likely to receive As in school compared to teens who had a family dinner two or fewer times a week (20% vs. 12%)

1. What effect did eating dinner with their families five nights or more have on teens?

   Teens who eat with their families five nights or more are more likely to avoid smoking and alcohol and to do better in school.

2. Which of the two strategies did you use to answer question 1?

   Possible response: I used "Think and Search" because the information came from two different sentences.

B. Return to the passage above, and circle the words or sentences that gave you the answer to the first question.

EQ How Do Families Affect Us?
Learn about the impact of family meals.

Do Family Meals Matter?

A. In "Do Family Meals Matter?" you found out how family meals affect teens. Use the information in the research report to complete the web.

Details Web

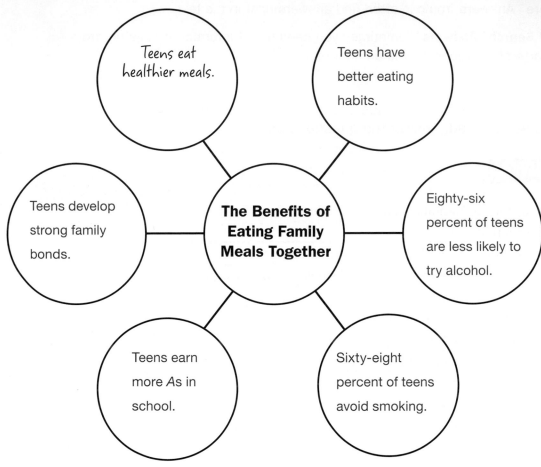

Teens eat healthier meals.

Teens have better eating habits.

Teens develop strong family bonds.

The Benefits of Eating Family Meals Together

Eighty-six percent of teens are less likely to try alcohol.

Teens earn more As in school.

Sixty-eight percent of teens avoid smoking.

B. Use the information in the web to answer the questions.

1. Why do the researchers believe families should eat together?

Family meals benefit teens. Teens eat better, avoid negative behavior such as smoking, and have stronger family bonds when they share family meals.

2. How do the authors use data in their report? Use **data** in your answer.

Possible response: The researchers use numerical data, such as statistics, to show that teens develop better health and behavior habits.

3. What are some more ways parents and teenagers could develop strong family bonds?

Possible response: Parents and teenagers could spend more time together by going to the movies or volunteering together.

Connect Across Texts

"Do Family Meals Matter?" discusses families eating together. In this anecdote, Amy Tan describes a memorable family meal.

FISH CHEEKS

BY AMY TAN

I fell in love with the minister's son the winter I turned fourteen. He was not Chinese, . . .

▲ The author, Amy Tan, has written numerous books including *The Joy Luck Club*, which was retold in a movie of the same name, and *The Chinese Siamese Cat*, which inspired the children's TV show "Sagwa."

Interact with the Text

1. Interpret
Look at the photo. Read the title, text, and "Connect Across Texts." What do you predict this anecdote will be about?

Possible response: Tan had a crush on a boy who was not Chinese. The family meal was probably memorable because he was not used to fish cheeks for dinner.

2. Anecdote
Remember that anecdotes focus on a single event. Circle the sentence that tells you what this anecdote will be about. What hints that the story is true?

The pronoun _I_ hints that

the story is true.

3. Anecdote
How does Tan describe the food? Explain why Tan's description is both humorous and terrifying.

Tan's description is

humorous and scary

because she describes

it as disgusting, inedible,

and about to come to life.

but as white as Mary in the manger. For Christmas I prayed for this blond-haired boy, Robert, and a slim new American nose.

When I found out that my parents had invited the minister's family over for Christmas Eve dinner, I cried. What would Robert think of our **shabby** Chinese Christmas? What would he think of our noisy Chinese relatives who lacked proper American manners? What terrible disappointment would he feel upon seeing not a roasted turkey and sweet potatoes but Chinese food?

On Christmas Eve, I saw that my mother had outdone herself in creating a strange menu. She was pulling black veins out of the backs of fleshy prawns. The kitchen was littered with **appalling** mounds of raw food: A slimy rock cod with bulging fish eyes that **pleaded** not to be thrown into a pan of hot oil. Tofu, which looked like stacked wedges of rubbery white sponges. A bowl soaking dried **fungus** back to life. A plate of squid, crisscrossed with knife markings so they resembled bicycle tires.

prawns or shrimp

tofu

And then they arrived—the minister's family and all my relatives in a clamor of doorbells and rumpled Christmas packages. Robert grunted hello, and I pretended he was not **worthy of existence**.

Dinner threw me deeper into **despair**. My relatives licked the ends of their chopsticks and reached across the table, dipping into the

In Other Words
shabby low-quality
appalling terrible
pleaded begged
fungus mushrooms
worthy of existence important to me

dozen or so plates of food. Robert and his family waited patiently for platters to be passed to them. My relatives murmured with pleasure when my mother brought out the whole steamed fish. Robert **grimaced**. Then my father <u>poked his chopsticks just below the fish eye</u> and <u>plucked out the soft meat</u>. "Amy, your favorite," he said, offering me the tender fish cheek. I wanted to disappear.

At the end of the meal my father leaned back and <u>belched loudly</u>, thanking my mother for her fine cooking. "It's a polite Chinese custom, to show you are satisfied," he explained to our astonished guests. Robert was looking down at his plate with a reddened face. The minister managed to muster a quiet burp. I was stunned into silence for the rest of the night.

After all the guests had gone, my mother said to me, "You want be same like American girls on the outside." She handed me an early gift. It was a miniskirt in beige tweed. "But inside, you must always be Chinese. You must be proud you different. **You only shame is be ashame.**"

The minister managed to muster a quiet burp.

And even though I didn't agree with her then, I knew that she understood how much I had suffered during the evening's dinner.

In Other Words
grimaced made an unhappy expression
You only shame is be ashame. The only thing you should be embarrassed about is that you are embarrassed.

4. Find Question-Answer Relationships
On pages 60 and 61, underline the phrases that explain why Tan was so ashamed of her family customs. Write a question you would like to ask the author. How do you think Tan would answer?

Possible response: Why didn't Tan ask her family to behave differently? It's possible that to ask that might have been disrespectful.

5. Interpret
What is Tan's mother trying to make her understand?

Tan's mother wants Tan to be proud of her Chinese background and her traditions. Her mother realizes how embarrassed Tan was at dinner, but she is telling Tan that she should never be ashamed of who she is.

6. Find Question-Answer Relationships

Underline the sentence that explains why Tan's mother made this specific meal. How do you feel about Tan's family now?

Possible response: It shows that Tan's mother loved her very much. I do not find Tan's family funny anymore, but very loving and wise.

It wasn't until many years later—long after I had gotten over my crush on Robert—that I was able to **appreciate** fully her lesson and the true purpose behind our particular menu. <u>For Christmas Eve that year, she had chosen all my favorite foods.</u> ❖

Key Vocabulary
- **appreciate** *v.*, to understand that something is good, to act grateful for it, to value it

Selection Review Fish Cheeks

A. Look through "Fish Cheeks" again. Write a question and answer in the chart for both types of Question-Answer relationships.

Relationship	Question	Answer
Author and Me	*Possible response:* How does the dinner affect Tan's relationship with her mother?	*Possible response:* The dinner eventually brings them closer together.
On My Own	*Possible response:* Why would people be embarrassed by their own family or customs?	*Possible response:* Family customs can seem unusual to people who do not understand them.

B. Answer the questions.

1. How does Tan's use of descriptive language help you understand her anecdote about Christmas Eve dinner?

Tan describes the food as disgusting and unusual. These descriptions help me understand why she felt so embarrassed in front of Robert.

2. Which details from the meal would you remember most vividly ten years from now?

Possible response: I might remember Robert's facial expressions when dinner was served.

Reflect and Assess

WRITING: Write About Literature

A. Plan your writing. Write what you liked and disliked about the two selections in the chart below. *Answers will vary.*

	Do Family Meals Matter?	Fish Cheeks
Likes		
Dislikes		

B. Which selection held your interest more? Why? Write a critical review. Support your review with information from the chart.

Students should support their answers with examples from the selections.

_____

_____

_____

_____

_____

_____

_____

_____

_____

Integrate the Language Arts

LITERARY ANALYSIS: Analyze Descriptive Language

Writers use **descriptive language** to help their readers picture characters, objects, and places. When writers use descriptive language, they appeal to the five senses. *Answers will vary. Possible responses are shown.*

A. Read the examples of descriptive language from "Fish Cheeks." Then describe how each helped you to picture the scene.

Description	The Picture I See
"The kitchen was littered with appalling mounds of raw food."	"Littered" and "appalling" show Tan did not enjoy preparing a traditional Chinese meal.
"At the end of the meal my father leaned back and belched loudly . . ."	In American culture it is rude to belch at the dinner table. This must have made Tan feel embarrassed.
"My relatives licked the ends of their chopsticks . . ."	This shows that the characters are eating one of their favorite meals and enjoying it very much.
"Tofu, which looked like stacked wedges of rubbery white sponges."	This helps the reader imagine what tofu must look like to a person who has never eaten it.

B. Read the sentences from "Fish Cheeks" below. Write which of the five senses they appeal to.

1. Then my father poked his chopsticks just below the fish eye and plucked out the soft meat. _sight, sound_

2. I was stunned into silence for the rest of the night. _sound, sight_

3. She handed me an early gift. It was a miniskirt in beige tweed. _touch, sight_

4. What terrible disappointment would he feel upon seeing not a roasted turkey and sweet potatoes but Chinese food? _sight, smell_

C. Write about a memorable meal you have had. Use descriptive language that appeals to the five senses.

Students should support their answers with language that appeals to the five senses.

VOCABULARY STUDY: Context Clues

Context clues are the words and phrases that surround an unfamiliar word and help you figure out the meaning of the unfamiliar word. One type of context clue is an example. Words that signal an example include *such as, including, like,* and *for example*.

A. Circle the context clues that helped you find the meanings of the words and phrases below. Then write what you think the underlined words or phrases mean.

Sentence(s) from the Text	What the Words/Phrases Mean
"Young people are more likely to avoid <u>problem behavior</u>, such as drug or alcohol use, the more their parents are involved in their lives."	bad habits
"Eating together more often was linked to <u>better eating habits.</u> This included eating more fruits and vegetables, less fried food, and fewer soft drinks."	healthier ways to eat
"They gave a <u>variety</u> of reasons, including indifference, lack of time, and arguing and fighting at the dinner table."	many

B. Complete the sentences. *Answers will vary. Possible responses are shown.*

1. A person might try to avoid problem behavior because ___it can lead to bad habits and interfere with___ success.

2. By choosing better eating habits ___a person can live a healthier life.___

3. There are a variety of ways to be healthy including ___getting lots of exercise and eating well.___

C. Use the words and phrases you learned to write a paragraph about the importance of eating healthy meals.

   Answers will vary. Possible responses should include the words and phrases above.

Prepare to Read

▸ Only Daughter
▸ Calling a Foul

Key Vocabulary

A. How well do you know these words? Circle a rating for each word. Check your understanding of each word by circling *yes* or *no*. Then, complete the sentences. If you are unsure of a word's meaning, refer to the Vocabulary Glossary, page 764, in your student text.

	Rating Scale
1	I have never seen this word before.
2	I am not sure of the word's meaning.
3	I know this word and can teach the word's meaning to someone else.

Key Word	Check Your Understanding	Deepen Your Understanding
❶ abusive (u-**byū**-siv) *adjective* **Rating:** 1　2　3	An **abusive** action is helpful. Yes　　(No)	Companies that are abusive to the environment _____ *Possible response:* pollute the air, land, and water _____ _____ _____ .
❷ approval (u-**prü**-vul) *noun* **Rating:** 1　2　3	In American society, nodding your head in agreement is a sign of **approval**. (Yes)　　No	I would give my approval if a classmate wanted to _____ *Possible response:* raise money for a good cause _____ _____ _____ .
❸ behavior (bi-**hā**-vyur) *noun* **Rating:** 1　2　3	People's **behavior** is what they say and do. (Yes)　　No	I was proud of my friend's behavior when _____ *Possible response:* she told the truth _____ _____ _____ .
❹ circumstance (**sur**-kum-stans) *noun* **Rating:** 1　2　3	It would be a lucky **circumstance** if someone returned your lost backpack. (Yes)　　No	One circumstance that can affect my schoolwork is _____ *Possible response:* doing homework late at night _____ _____ _____ .

Key Word	Check Your Understanding	Deepen Your Understanding
5 **destiny** (**des**-tu-nē) *noun* **Rating:** 1 2 3	Everyone has exactly the same **destiny** in life. Yes (No)	I think it is my destiny to *Possible response:* go to college _____ _____ _____ .
6 **embarrass** (im-**bair**-us) *verb* **Rating:** 1 2 3	If you **embarrass** a friend, you make him feel happy and proud. Yes (No)	Sometimes I embarrass my family when I _____ *Possible response:* tell a bad joke _____ _____ .
7 **role** (**rōl**) *noun* **Rating:** 1 2 3	Most actors want a leading **role** in a play. (Yes) No	The most important role I play in my family is _____ *Possible response:* babysitter _____ _____ .
8 **valuable** (**val**-yū-bul) *adjective* **Rating:** 1 2 3	Something that is **valuable** has no worth. Yes (No)	Something that is not valuable to me anymore is _____ *Possible response:* my broken CD player _____ _____ .

B. In what ways can parents affect their children? Use one of the Key Vocabulary words in your answer.

Answers will vary. _____

_____

Before Reading Only Daughter

LITERARY ELEMENT: Memoir

A **memoir** tells about a specific time in the writer's life and is told in the writer's own words. It includes:

- details about people and events
- why the people and events are important to the writer

A. Read the passage below. Find the clues that tell you this is a memoir. Complete the chart.

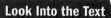
Look Into the Text

> Once, several years ago, when I was just starting out my writing career, I was asked to write my own contributor's note for an anthology I was part of. I wrote: "I am the only daughter in a family of six sons. *That* explains everything."
>
> Well, I've thought about that ever since, and yes, it explains a lot to me, but for the reader's sake I should have written: "I am the only daughter in a *Mexican* family of six sons." Or even: "I am the only daughter of a Mexican father and a Mexican-American mother." Or: "I am the only daughter of a working-class family of nine." All of these had everything to do with who I am today.

Elements of a Memoir	Clues from Passage
Event	The writer remembers writing a note about herself as an only daughter.
People	The writer has six brothers, a Mexican father, and a Mexican American mother.
Importance of event and people	This event is important because it makes her think about how she sees herself and how being a part of her family has made her who she is.

B. What will you will learn about the writer after reading her memoir?

I will probably learn what it was like for the writer to grow up in a Mexican-American family, how difficult it was to have six brothers, and what it was like to be working-class.

READING STRATEGY: Question the Author

How to Question the Author

1. **Use a Double-Entry Journal** Write questions for the author in one column of a two-column chart.

2. **Answer Your Question** Answer the questions as you read on. The answer may be right there.

3. **Think Beyond the Text** Use what you already know from your life and the author's life to answer questions.

A. Read the passage. Use the strategies above to question the author as you read. Answer the questions below.

Look Into the Text

> Being only a daughter for my father meant my destiny would lead me to become someone's wife. That's what he believed. But when I was in fifth grade and shared my plans for college with him, I was sure he understood. I remember my father saying, "*Que bueno, mi'ja,* that's good." That meant a lot to me, especially since my brothers thought the idea hilarious. What I didn't realize was that my father thought college was good for girls—for finding a husband.

1. Write a question for the author.

   Possible response: What does "being only a daughter for my father" mean?

2. Think beyond the text, and answer your question.

   Possible response: I think the writer means that her father saw her as someone's future wife and nothing else.

B. How did the reading strategy help you answer your question?

   Possible response: I thought about my own life experiences and what it must have been like to be the only daughter in a family of boys.

Selection Review Only Daughter

EQ ## How Do Families Affect Us?
Read about how the behavior of parents can make a difference.

A. In "Only Daughter," you found out how the behavior of a parent can affect other family members. Complete the chart below about Cisneros's father and how his actions and beliefs affected her.

Cause-and-Effect Chart

Father's Actions and Beliefs	How It Affects Cisneros
He thinks college is for finding a husband.	She studies English instead of looking for a wealthy man to marry.
He introduces her as a teacher.	She realizes her father does not understand how important writing is to her. This makes her want his approval.
He believes only a few types of books and magazines are worth reading.	She thinks that she writes for an audience that does not care about her kind of writing.
He announces he has seven sons.	She feels worthless.
He reads a story she wrote about his neighborhood and wants copies for the whole family.	She feels wonderful.

B. Use the information in the chart to answer the questions.

1. Why is most of Cisneros's memoir about her father?

   His actions and beliefs strongly affected her life and writing.

2. When does Cisneros finally feel like she had gained her father's approval? Use **approval** in your answer.

   Her father showed his approval after he read her story about his old neighborhood. He wanted to give copies to his relatives.

3. How might Cisneros's life have been different if her father had encouraged her to become a writer?

   Possible response: She might have written about different topics not connected to her family.

Connect Across Texts

In "Only Daughter," Sandra Cisneros describes how her father affected her life. In this news commentary, Stan Simpson tells how other parents have an impact on their children.

STAN SIMPSON

Calling a Foul

Bill Cardarelli was impressed by a high school basketball player. He thought she would be a fine addition to the St. Joseph College women's team he coached.

Then he saw her dad in action as **a spectator**.

"He was absolutely bad-mouthing the coach," Cardarelli recalled. "I mean yelling: 'You don't know how to coach! What are you doing?' "

The kid was no longer that **valuable** to Cardarelli.

"I stopped **recruiting her**," he said. "Because you knew what was **in line for** the next coach to get that guy."

Bad-behaving parents at sports events have become a painful reality.

The stuff that happens after the game is just as shocking. A Connecticut parent spit at a high school basketball coach because he didn't like how the coach was coaching. Referees and coaches have been physically attacked after school games. And it's not unusual for parents to be banned from a game until they can control their emotions.

State high school athletic directors say it is more difficult than ever to attract coaches and game officials. They're not willing to put up with **abusive** parents.

Now there's a bill that would make it a crime to attack a sports official at a game.

Time-out.

Has it really come to this? Do we need a law to remind adults that they should act like grownups at sports events?

"That's a sad **commentary**," said John Shukie, president of the Connecticut Association of Athletic Directors. "It's kind of **an indictment of** where sports have been going in our society. The importance people place

Key Vocabulary
valuable adj., having worth, important
abusive adj., hurtful, cruel, harsh

In Other Words
a spectator someone watching the game
recruiting her trying to get her to join my team
in line for going to happen to
commentary statement about the issue
an indictment of a negative comment about

Interact with the Text

1. News Commentary
Underline the author's opinions in the first column. What is he trying to tell the reader?

A young athlete is not

worth recruiting if a

parent behaves badly at

games or with the coach.

Parents' behavior is

ruining sports.

2. News Commentary
Circle three facts in the second column. How do you know these are facts and not opinions?

You could find this same

information in other news

articles. It can be proved.

3. Interpret
Underline the reason the author thinks parents behave rudely at sporting events. What effect does this ultimately have on their children?

Possible response:

Children are embarrassed

by their parents.

Ultimately, parents

embarrass themselves.

4. Question the Author
Circle what the writer thinks should be done to repeat offenders. How does he view these parents' behavior? How does he support his opinion?

Possible response: The

writer thinks their behavior

is embarrassing and it

makes them bad parents.

Throughout the article

he shows how parents'

behavior can negatively

affect their children.

on winning and losing is greater than ever now."

The small percentage of **overzealous** parents out there has become an unwelcome part of youth athletics. You can't stop these parents. You can only hope to keep them under control. <u>Many want their children to be successful athletes so badly that they don't notice their kids are NOT good enough to get athletic scholarships.</u> It doesn't matter how many trophies their kids won in sports when they were really little. The parents **embarrass** themselves and their kids with their angry performances.

"We have lost our sense of **decorum**," says athletic director June Bernabucci of Hartford. "Parents and all adults have to stop **living vicariously through** their children and their sports activities."

No law in the world will stop a fuming parent from fighting with a coach or an official. But every parent of a student athlete should sign an agreement that outlines consequences for his or her bad **behavior**:

- I will not confront a coach or sports official after a game ends.

- I will not shout insults at other athletes on either team.

- I will not use **profanity**.

- I will sit in the stands, support the team, and pretend that I'm the adult.

Yeah, maybe it's a little childish. But wait until you hear the consequences.

Repeat offenders would be **banned** from games, unless they wear a huge sign: *As a parent, I stink.* ❖

Key Vocabulary
embarrass *v.*, to make someone feel confused, uneasy, or ashamed
behavior *n.*, the way a person acts, conduct

In Other Words
overzealous extreme, intense
decorum good behavior
living vicariously through pushing their own dreams on
profanity bad words
banned kept away from

About the Writer

Stan Simpson (1962–) writes a weekly column for the *Hartford Courant*, a newspaper in Hartford, Connecticut. He also hosts a weekly news radio program. His work addresses a wide range of issues, including education, criminal justice, and local politics.

Key Vocabulary
- **role** *n.*, a part you play on stage or in real life

Interact with the Text

5. Interpret
Underline the issues the author writes about. Why do you think the author writes about this issue?

Possible response:

The author writes

about education, so he

probably sees the effects

parents' behavior has on

school sports.

Selection Review Calling a Foul

A. Choose one opinion and one fact from the article. Use the strategies to question the author.

Fact: *Possible response:* There is a bill that would make it a crime to attack a coach.

Question: *Possible response:* Has anyone ever been arrested? Has the bill helped?

Opinion: *Possible response:* No law in the world will stop an angry parent.

Question: *Possible response:* Why do you think that? Can you justify this?

1. How did questioning the author help you understand the text better?

Questioning the author helped me understand which is fact and which is the author's opinion. It also showed me how the author used facts to support his opinion.

Selection Review continued

B. The author writes his opinion about parents' behavior at sports events, but he also includes facts. Complete the T chart, separating the article's facts and opinions. Then answer the questions below.

T Chart

Facts	Opinions
A Connecticut parent spit at a basketball coach.	Parents should have to sign an agreement.
High school athletic directors have difficulty finding coaches and officials.	Repeat offenders should be banned.

1. How did identifying the facts and opinions in this news commentary help you understand the text?

It was helpful to separate facts from opinions so I could form my own ideas about the topic.

_____

2. This news commentary focused on the bad behavior of some parents. What do you think those parents would say about this news commentary? Write a paragraph.

Possible response: They would probably say they are just supporting their kids and making sure that

the coaches are doing what they are supposed to be doing.

_____

_____

_____

_____

_____

_____

_____

_____

_____

_____

Reflect and Assess

WRITING: Write About Literature

A. Write three things parents do to support their children in a positive way. Provide examples from one or both texts to support each item.

Answers will vary. Possible responses are shown.

> **Positive Things Parents Can Do**
>
> **1.** Listen to your children and respect the choices they make. In "Only Daughter," Cisneros's father finally read her writing, and it made her feel good.
>
> **2.** Support your children's dreams and goals, not your own. The parents in "Calling a Foul" want their children to become professional athletes, but that is the parents' dream and not the child's.
>
> **3.** Act like a mature, responsible adult. Yelling at a coach or even becoming physically abusive is immature and can only cause harm.

B. Use the examples you listed from both texts to write a short guide for parents.

Students should support their answers with examples from both selections.

Integrate the Language Arts

LITERARY ANALYSIS: Analyze Style

The words that authors choose and the way these words are arranged create the author's **style** of writing. Style may change depending on the form, or genre, and the effect the author wants to have on the readers.

A. Read the excerpt from "Calling a Foul." Circle any words or phrases that indicate the author's direct, informal style.

> "(You) can't stop these parents. (You) can only hope to keep them under control. Many want their children to be successful athletes (so badly) that they don't notice their kids are (NOT good enough) to get athletic scholarships. (It doesn't matter) how many trophies their (kids) won in sports when they (were really little)."

B. Write the examples that you circled and which element of style the author is using. *Answers will vary. Possible responses are shown.*

Examples from the Text	Author's Style
author's use of *you*	uses second-person pronoun *you*
so badly; *not good enough*; *It doesn't matter*; *kids*; *were really little*	uses informal words and phrases
Some sentences are long, as if the author is talking to a friend.	arranges the words using his own style
NOT	draws attention to language in other ways

C. Imagine that you are the child of one of the parents the author describes. Write a letter to your parent. Use the same style of writing as this author.

Answers will vary. Students' letters should match the author's direct and informal style.

_____

_____

_____

_____

_____

_____

_____

_____

VOCABULARY STUDY: Context Clues

Synonyms are words that have about the same meaning. **Antonyms** are words that have the opposite meaning. **Context clues** with synonyms and antonyms can help you figure out the meanings of unfamiliar words.

A. Read each example from "Calling a Foul" and circle a synonym or antonym for the underlined word or phrase.

1. "'He was absolutely bad-mouthing the coach,' Cardarelli recalled. 'I mean (yelling.) . . .'"

2. "'That's a (sad commentary) . . . It's kind of an indictment of where sports have been going in our society.'"

3. "The small percentage of overzealous parents out there has become an unwelcome part of youth athletics. . . . You can only hope to keep them (under control.)"

4. "No law in the world will stop a fuming parent from (fighting) with a coach or an official."

B. Write what you think each word or phrase means based on the context clues you circled above.

Word or Phrase	What It Means
bad-mouthing	to yell or say bad things
fuming	angry
indictment	a negative comment
overzealous	out of control or extreme

C. Now that you know each word's meaning, write sentences using the words below. *Answers will vary.*

bad-mouthing _____

_____

fuming _____

_____

indictment _____

_____

overzealous _____

_____

Key Vocabulary Review

A. Read each sentence. Circle the word that best fits into each sentence.

1. Locking up your bike is an example of protecting (**valuable**)/ **beneficial**) property.

2. Each person has (**united** /(**unique**)) characteristics.

3. A recipe follows a specific (**sequence**)/ **trait**) of steps.

4. People are (**united**)/ **abusive**) when they all work together.

5. Scientists collect (**circumstances** /(**data**)) when they do experiments.

6. You need a microscope to study a (**molecule**)/ **survey**).

7. People use e-mail to (**inherit** /(**transmit**)) information.

8. An archaeologist may have to perform an (**extraction**)/ **approval**) to remove artifacts from the ground.

B. Use your own words to write what each Key Vocabulary word means. Then write a synonym for each word. *Answers will vary. Possible responses are shown.*

Key Word	My Definition	Synonym
1. **approval**	agreeing to something	acceptance
2. **beneficial**	helpful	favorable
3. **control**	to rule or have power	direct
4. **destiny**	what will happen in the future	fate
5. **embarrass**	to humiliate someone	upset
6. **research**	a study to find facts	investigation
7. **role**	a part someone plays	function
8. **trait**	a distinguishing feature	characteristic

Unit 2 Key Vocabulary

abusive	• beneficial	control	• extraction	• role	• transmit
• appreciate	• bond	• data	inherit	• sequence	• unique
approval	• circumstance	destiny	molecule	• survey	united
behavior	• consume	embarrass	• research	trait	valuable

• **Academic Vocabulary**

C. Answer the questions using complete sentences. *Answers will vary. Possible responses are shown.*

1. Why might someone conduct a **survey**?

He or she might want to learn about other people's thoughts and opinions.

2. Describe a **circumstance** that might make you late for something.

Snow or rain might make me late.

3. Describe a time when your **behavior** changed what people thought of you.

I began to study a lot. People began to think I was serious and smart.

4. What person do you **appreciate** the most?

I appreciate my mom the most.

5. Who do you have a special **bond** with?

I have a special bond with my sister.

6. What is your favorite food to **consume**?

I like to consume tacos.

7. What qualities did you **inherit** from a family member?

I inherited my brown eyes and curly hair from my father.

8. Why do animal shelters rescue pets from **abusive** owners?

Abusive owners do not take good care of their pets.

Prepare to Read
▶ Heartbeat
▶ Behind the Bulk

Key Vocabulary

A. How well do you know these words? Circle a rating for each word. Check your understanding of each word by marking an X next to the correct definition. Then complete the sentences. If you are unsure of a word's meaning, refer to the Vocabulary Glossary, page 764, in your student text.

Rating Scale	
1	I have never seen this word before.
2	I am not sure of the word's meaning.
3	I know this word and can teach the word's meaning to someone else.

Key Word	Check Your Understanding	Deepen Your Understanding
1 appearance (u-**pear**-uns) *noun* **Rating:** 1 2 3	☐ a person's actions ☒ the way a person looks	One way to change your appearance is _____ *Possible response:* to dye your hair .
2 depressed (di-**prest**) *adjective* **Rating:** 1 2 3	☐ happy and charming ☒ sad and gloomy	To cheer up a friend who is depressed, you can _____ *Possible response:* spend time with her doing her favorite things .
3 distorted (di-**stor**-ted) *adjective* **Rating:** 1 2 3	☐ true and accurate ☒ not true and not real	An object can look distorted if you _____ *Possible response:* look at it through water .
4 illusion (i-**lü**-zhun) *noun* **Rating:** 1 2 3	☒ something that is not real ☐ something that is hard to find	One example of an illusion I have seen is _____ *Possible response:* the image of a ghost at a haunted house .

Key Word	Check Your Understanding	Deepen Your Understanding
5 normal (**nor**-mul) *adjective* **Rating:** 1 2 3	[X] usual or regular [ ] unnatural or irregular	On a normal weekend, I like to _Possible response:_ hang out with my friends _____ _____ _____ .
6 solution (su-**lü**-shun) *noun* **Rating:** 1 2 3	[X] the act of solving a problem [ ] the act of cleaning	When I have trouble finding a solution to a problem, I ___ _Possible response:_ ask my mom for advice _____ _____ _____ .
7 transform (trans-**form**) *verb* **Rating:** 1 2 3	[ ] to copy [X] to change	One way to transform an empty room is to _____ _Possible response:_ add furniture _____ _____ _____ .
8 weight (wāt) *noun* **Rating:** 1 2 3	[ ] a measurement of diameter [X] a measurement of heaviness	One way to lose weight is to _Possible response:_ exercise _____ _____ _____ .

B. Use one of the Key Vocabulary words to write about a time you learned something new about yourself.

Answers will vary.

_____

_____

Before Reading Heartbeat

LITERARY ANALYSIS: Point of View

A first-person narrator tells the story using *I*, *me*, and *my*. A first-person narrator describes characters and events from his or her **point of view**.

A. Read the passage below. Complete the chart with the thoughts and feelings that tell you each character's point of view.

> ### Look Into the Text
>
> My nickname's "Heartbeat," because my friends swear that you can actually see the pulse on my bare chest. I've always been skinny. Everyone assumes I'm a weakling because I'm so thin (I prefer "lean and mean" or "wiry"), despite being a three-sport athlete. I decided to do something about it this fall when Sarah, the girl I have a crush on, said "Oh my God . . . you are so skinny." She was visibly repulsed by my sunken chest as I stepped off the soccer bus after practice. I silently vowed to do everything within my power to become the "after" picture. I was sixteen years old, but looked like I was eleven.

Character	Character's Thoughts and Feelings
"Heartbeat"	knows he's not a weakling will do whatever it takes to look bigger to impress Sarah thinks he is lean and mean and wiry
Sarah	is disgusted by Heartbeat's sunken chest

B. Answer the questions about the characters' points of view.

Does appearance matter to Heartbeat, the narrator? To Sarah? Why or why not?

Possible response: Appearance matters to both Sarah and the narrator. The narrator wants to change his appearance for Sarah, and Sarah doesn't like that Heartbeat is so skinny.

READING STRATEGY: Make Inferences

HOW TO MAKE INFERENCES

1. You Read Look for clues in the text.

2. You Know Think about what your experience tells you.

3. And So Combine what you already know with what you read to make an inference.

A. Use the strategies to make inferences as you read. Complete the chart.

Look Into the Text

> For the rest of the fall, <u>I did countless push-ups and curled free weights</u> until I couldn't bend my arms. I got ridiculously strong and defined, but I wasn't gaining weight. I wanted to be *thicker.* I didn't care about getting stronger if nobody could tell. <u>I did research, and started lifting heavier weights at lower reps</u> and <u>supplemented my meals with weight-gainer shakes, egg whites, boiled yams, and tubs of cottage cheese.</u>

You Read	You Know	And So
"I did countless push-ups and curled free weights"	Lifting weights usually makes you bigger.	The narrator wants to look bigger so Sarah will like him.
I did research, and started lifting weights at lower reps	*Possible response:* When you lift weights differently you get different results.	*Possible response:* He cares about looking bigger, not being stronger.

1. What inference can you make about the narrator?

Possible response: The narrator doesn't care how he gains weight and will try anything to look bigger.

2. How did using the strategy help you understand the text better?

Possible response: By thinking about my own experiences with weight training, I know that all of these things the narrator is doing are difficult to do.

B. Underline the clues that helped you make your inference.

Selection Review Heartbeat

Do We Find or Create Our True Selves?
Explore whether appearance matters.

A. In "Heartbeat," the narrator, Dave, decides to change his appearance to make someone else like him. Write what Dave does in the chart.

Why Dave Wants to Change	What Dave Does to Change
Sarah tells him he is skinny.	Dave works out but does not gain weight.
People begin to notice Dave's muscle growth.	Dave adds layers of clothing so that people think he is even bigger.
Dave becomes ill from all of the layers of clothing.	Dave decides to stop trying to become bigger and be himself.

B. Use the information in the chart to answer the questions.

1. Why does Dave begin to wear T-shirts under his sweaters and shirts?

   He thinks wearing them makes him look stronger, and he hopes Sarah will like him more if he looks bigger.

2. Why doesn't his solution work? Use **solution** in your answer.

   Possible response: The narrator's solution doesn't work because wearing so many layers of clothing makes it difficult for him to move and breathe.

3. Do you think he will feel differently about his appearance in the future? Why or why not?

   Possible response: Yes, he will start to feel differently when he gets older because he may realize that looks are not that important. He also might start to grow naturally and will no longer have to pretend to look bigger.

Behind the Bulk

BY CATE BAILY

Connect Across Texts

In "Heartbeat," Dave learns to accept the way he looks. Read this informative article about a young man who tries to build up his body.

Every time he passed a mirror, Craig flexed his muscles. He wanted to look "insanely big—like an action figure."

"When I walked into a room, I wanted **heads to turn**," he says. People did notice Craig's 225-pound, 5-foot 9-inch **frame**. But what they didn't see was the physical damage and **psychological turmoil** going on inside.

The story behind the bulk was five years of **steroid abuse** and a struggle with muscle dysmorphia. Muscle dysmorphia is a condition in which a person has a **distorted** image of his or her body. Men with this condition think that they look small and weak, even if they are large and muscular.

Illegal and Grim

It all started when Craig was 18. Before a summer trip to Orlando, Florida, he was feeling overweight. He wanted to look good, so he resolved to get fit. Running on the treadmill, he slimmed down fast, losing 20 pounds in a month.

But lean wasn't Craig's ideal. "I wanted people to say, 'That guy's huge.'" He lifted **weights** and experimented with steroidal **supplements**, also called dietary supplements. These drugs promise to build muscles. Despite <u>potential risks and unclear effectiveness,</u> they can be bought legally over the counter at many stores.

But what Craig was looking for couldn't be bought in a store. So he turned to anabolic steroids.

Anabolic steroids have some **legitimate** medical uses when taken under a doctor's supervision. But to use steroids for muscle-building in a healthy body is illegal. This didn't

Key Vocabulary

- **distorted** *adj.*, twisted out of shape, not representing the truth
- **weight** *n.*, heavy gym equipment used for exercising

In Other Words

heads to turn people to notice me
frame body
psychological turmoil mental confusion
steroid abuse incorrect use of a medical drug
supplements pills
legitimate real, valuable

Interact with the Text

1. Point of View
Circle a pronoun that tells you this informative article is written in third-person point of view. How has the writer incorporated Craig's thoughts and ideas?

The writer used

Craig's exact words in

quotations to show how

Craig felt.

2. Make Inferences
Underline a phrase that tells you why steroidal supplements are dangerous. What can you infer about why people take supplements?

Possible response: The

people who take the

supplements care more

about how big they look

than how dangerous the

supplements are.

3. Make Inferences

Underline words and phrases that describe Craig's relationships with other people. What can you infer about how Craig's struggle affected those relationships?

Possible response: Craig

was so focused on his

weight that he ruined

relationships with his

family and friends.

4. Point of View

Highlight facts that tell you the effects steroids had on Craig. Why did the author include the information?

Possible response:

The author wanted the

reader to understand

what Craig was doing to

his body and how much

damage steroids do.

---

stop Craig. Neither did the many **grim potential side effects**.

Craig thought he knew exactly what he was getting into. Like 4% of high school seniors and an

How Weight Training Builds Muscle

Muscle fibers contain long myofibrils, which are made up of strands of protein. When you lift weights, the protein strands get larger. This causes the muscle fibers to expand.

Muscle Before Training

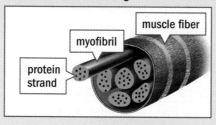

Muscle After Training

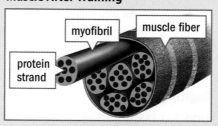

▲ **Interpret the Diagrams** Which part of a muscle fiber gets larger and causes the muscle fiber to expand?

---

estimated hundreds of thousands of adults, he took steroids anyway.

Heart Problems

Craig's **appearance** was that important to him. "The scale was my enemy. Every pound meant so much to me," he says.

Craig constantly compared himself to others. He drove his friends and family crazy asking, "Is that guy bigger than me? What about that guy?"

He never had complete satisfaction. "Some days, I'd be **arrogant**, wearing shorts to show off my quads. Other days, I'd be a disaster. On those days, I'd have to wear big, baggy clothes."

Craig's steroid use **escalated** over time. He had begun by taking oral steroids (pills) exclusively. But when he heard that injectable steroids were more effective, he overcame a fear of needles. At his worst, he was injecting three to four times and taking ten pills a day.

The drugs **took their toll**. Craig's hair fell out. Acne popped up all over his back. His face swelled. Then, something even more serious happened: he started having chest pains.

Key Vocabulary
appearance *n.*, the way someone or something looks

In Other Words
grim potential side effects other bad things the steroids could do to his body
arrogant really proud
escalated increased
took their toll hurt Craig's body

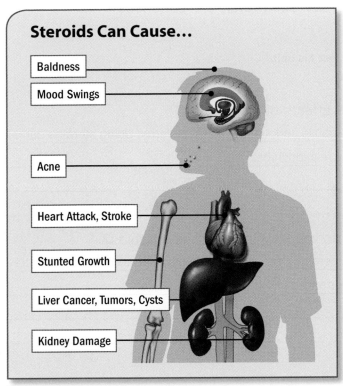

Steroids Can Cause...

- Baldness
- Mood Swings
- Acne
- Heart Attack, Stroke
- Stunted Growth
- Liver Cancer, Tumors, Cysts
- Kidney Damage

▲ **Interpret the Diagram** Name three problems that steroids can cause.

New Priorities

Craig was having other problems, too. Craig, then 25, was screaming and yelling at his wife a lot. Ultimately, his marriage ended. He <u>lost a **custody battle** over his 1-year-old son</u>, Jake. Craig's wife said that <u>Craig couldn't see their child until he passed a drug test.</u>

That was the moment when everything changed for Craig. He knew he had to quit.

On Father's Day, Craig **went cold turkey**. He knew he needed help, so his parents found him a psychiatrist, who treated him through **the better part of a** year.

Today, Craig's **priorities** have changed. He still wants to be a head-turner, but for a different reason. "Now I'd rather be walking into a room with my son and have people thinking, 'Wow, he's the greatest dad in the world.'" ❖

In Other Words
custody battle legal fight with his wife
went cold turkey completely quit taking steroids
the better part of a most of the
priorities values

5. Make Inferences
Underline phrases that tell why Craig decided to quit taking steroids. What can you infer about his decision?

Possible response:

Craig realized that being with his son was more important than looking muscular.

6. Point of View
Circle the sentence that tells what Craig wants people to notice about him now. Explain why the author ends the article with Craig's quote.

Possible response: The quote uses Craig's own words to show how much he has changed and what he thinks is most important now.

Selection Review Behind the Bulk

A. Read the two details from the article about Craig's experiences with steroids.

> **Detail 1:** Craig developed acne and lost his hair.
> **Detail 2:** Craig's marriage fell apart.

1. What can you infer about the effects of steroid use?

Possible response: Steroids can cause serious physical problems. Using steroids can also cause
emotional problems and damage relationships.

2. Based on Craig's story, why do you think people take steroids?

Possible response: People take steroids because they have a distorted view of how they look. They
think steroids will help them look better than other people.

B. Answer the questions.

1. How would the article be different if the information had been presented in the first-person rather than the third-person point of view?

Possible response: Much of the scientific research and background information about steroids would
not have been presented. The article would have been more about Craig's personal story rather than
an informative article about steroids.

2. What is your opinion about steroid use? Write a statement. Use at least two pieces of text evidence from the article.

Students should support their answer with examples from the selection.

Reflect and Assess

WRITING: Write About Literature

A. Plan your writing. List the reasons why Dave in "Heartbeat" and Craig in "Behind the Bulk" worry about how they look to others. *Answers will vary.*

Dave	Craig
Dave thinks his nickname, "Heartbeat," makes him sound weak.	Craig wanted people to notice him.

B. Why do people worry about how they look to others? Write a short explanation. Support your explanation with reasons Dave and Craig have from the chart.

People worry about how they look because *Students should support their explanations with reasons*

from both selections.

_____

_____

_____

_____

_____

_____

_____

_____

Integrate the Language Arts

LITERARY ANALYSIS: Analyze Point of View

In **third-person limited point of view**, the narrator describes the actions, thoughts, and feelings of a person or character. *Answers will vary. Possible responses are shown.*

A. In "Behind the Bulk," the information was told from a third-person limited point of view. Write Craig's actions, thoughts, and feelings in the chart below.

Actions	Thoughts	Feelings
compared himself to others turned to anabolic steroids started to take pills and use needles yelled at his wife wore shorts to show off his quads	he was huge	overcame a fear of needles felt bad about how his drug use affected his son

B. Choose one example from each column in the chart above. Rewrite each example from the point of view of the people listed below.

1. Craig's friends:

Craig was so annoying. He always asked if he was bigger or smaller than everyone else.

2. Craig's wife:

It was so hurtful the way Craig used to yell at me. The steroids made him an angry person.

3. Craig's son:

Now my dad is great. He does not yell anymore.

C. Explain how the article would have been different, for you as a reader, if the author had not used third-person limited point of view. How would you feel about Craig?

If the author had not used third-person limited point of view, I would know more about how Craig's family and friends felt. I might feel more upset with Craig for hurting the people he loved because I would know firsthand how his family and friends acted and felt. I may not have sympathized with Craig as much, or I might have missed some of the important information about steroids.

VOCABULARY STUDY: Word Families

Knowing the meaning of a word in a **word family** can help you understand the meaning of another word in the same family. For example, if you know that *appearance* means "the way you look," you might guess that *appear* means "to be seen." *Answers will vary. Possible responses are shown.*

A. Read each Key Vocabulary word in the chart. Write a word you know that is from the same word family. Then write what the related word means. Use a dictionary to check the meaning.

Key Vocabulary	Related Word	Definition
distorted	distort	twisted from its original meaning or shape
normal	norm	a standard or average
transform	transformation	the act of changing

B. Think of related words you know from each word family and list as many as you can in the chart.

Word	Related Words I Know
athletic	athlete, athleticism
escalated	escalator, escalate
opted	option, optional
ridiculous	ridiculously, ridiculousness, ridicule

C. Use one of the words you know from the chart above in a sentence. Check your sentences by confirming the meaning of each word in a dictionary.

1. I admire great athletes.

2. I have very little patience for ridiculousness.

3. I took the escalator to the top floor.

4. Homework is not optional.

Prepare to Read

▶ I Go Along
▶ Theme for English B

Key Vocabulary

A. How well do you know these words? Circle a rating for each word. Check your understanding of each word by circling the synonym. Then complete the sentences. If you are unsure of a word's meaning, refer to the Vocabulary Glossary, page 764, in your student text.

	Rating Scale
1	I have never seen this word before.
2	I am not sure of the word's meaning.
3	I know this word and can teach the word's meaning to someone else.

Key Word	Check Your Understanding	Deepen Your Understanding
❶ advanced (ud-**vanst**) *adjective* Rating: 1 2 3	An **advanced** class is a _____ class. (high-level) beginning	Someday I would like to take advanced classes in _____ *Possible response:* art and English
❷ category (**ca**-tu-gor-ē) *noun* Rating: 1 2 3	A **category** is a _____. individual (group)	My favorite category of music is _____ *Possible response:* hip-hop
❸ poet (pō-ut) *noun* Rating: 1 2 3	A **poet** is an _____. (author) historian	One poet that I really like is _____ *Possible response:* Langston Hughes
❹ potential (pu-**ten**-shul) *noun* Rating: 1 2 3	If you show **potential**, you show _____. inability (ability)	I think I have the potential to _____ *Possible response:* become a writer

Key Word	Check Your Understanding	Deepen Your Understanding
5 **program** (**prō**-gram) *noun* Rating: 1 2 3	A **program** is a _____. song (show)	I recently saw a TV program that was about _____ *Possible response:* my favorite actor _____ _____ _____.
6 **realize** (**rē**-u-līz) *verb* Rating: 1 2 3	To **realize** something is to _____ it. (know) guess at	I would like my teachers to realize that _____ *Possible response:* exams don't always tell them how smart a student is _____ _____ _____.
7 **serious** (**sear**-ē-us) *adjective* Rating: 1 2 3	A **serious** person is _____. (thoughtful) amusing	The times I am most serious are when _____ *Possible response:* I am studying or reading a book _____ _____ _____.
8 **understand** (un-dur-**stand**) *verb* Rating: 1 2 3	To **understand** something is to _____ it. misinterpret (comprehend)	If I had to talk about something I understand, it would be *Possible response:* my hobby _____ _____ _____.

B. Use two of the Key Vocabulary words to tell something about yourself.

Answers will vary. _____

_____

Selection Review I Go Along

Do We Find or Create Our True Selves?
Find out about people who put themselves in categories.

A. In "I Go Along," you read how Gene's field trip makes him question his real potential. Write what happens on the field trip and what it shows about each character in the Character Description Map.

Character Description Map

Character	What the Character Says and Thinks	What This Shows About the Character
Gene	Gene thinks his teacher knows no one in his class will go to the reading. Gene can't believe Sharon is sitting next to him.	Gene thinks he understands the feelings of his classmates. Gene thinks Sharon belongs with the smart students and wouldn't want to sit with him.
	Gene asks Sharon what she will write about.	Gene is curious about Sharon.
	Gene wonders what it would be like to be in Sharon's advanced class.	Gene wants to be part of the smart group.
Sharon	Sharon refuses to sit with her friends on the bus. Sharon tells Gene he is smart.	Sharon wants to sit with Gene. Sharon likes Gene.

B. Use the information in the map to answer the questions.

1. Why do you think Gene decides to go on the field trip to the poetry reading?

Possible response: Gene probably wants to challenge himself and be a part of the smart group of students in the advanced class.

2. Does Gene have more potential than he believes he does? Why or why not? Use the word **potential** in your response.

Possible response: Gene has more potential than he thinks he does because he is smart, according to Sharon. He is interested in bettering himself and is curious about how Sharon, an advanced student, will respond to the reading.

3. How will Gene's experience at the poetry reading and with Sharon change him?

Possible response: Gene will probably be a better student in the future. He no longer wants to be in his class and is already thinking that it would be more interesting to be in the advanced class. Sharon might be a good influence on him, too.

Connect Across Texts
In "I Go Along," Gene thinks about how people fit in at school. In this poem, the speaker also thinks about **categories** of people.

Theme for
English B
by Langston Hughes

The instructor said,

    Go home and write

    a page tonight.

    And let that page come out of you —

5   *Then, it will be true.*

I wonder if it's that simple?

I am twenty-two, colored, born in Winston-Salem.

I went to school there, then Durham, then here

to this college on the hill above Harlem.

10 I am the only colored student in my class.

The steps from the hill lead down into Harlem,

through a park, then I cross St. Nicholas,

Eighth Avenue, Seventh, and I come to the Y,

the Harlem Branch Y, where I take the elevator

15 up to my room, sit down, and write this page:

It's not easy to know what is true for you or me

at twenty-two, my age. But I guess I'm what

Key Vocabulary
- **category** *n.*, a group of items that are similar in some way

Interact with the Text

1. Poetry
Reread lines 1–5. How do you know you are reading a poem and not a short story?

The text is arranged in

lines, and the words

have rhythm.

2. Poetry
Reread lines 6–15. Circle clues that tell you about the speaker. What is the speaker like?

Possible response: The

speaker is not sure who

he is yet, but he knows

this is what others see.

3. Make Inferences

Reread lines 18–19. What is an important part of the speaker's identity? Explain the speaker's message in your own words.

Possible response: The

speaker is saying that

the sights, sounds, and

feelings of Harlem are

all part of his identity.

Harlem is his world.

4. Poetry

Reread lines 20–35. Underline words that tell you who the audience is. Is there more than one audience? Explain.

The audience is the

white instructor, but he

is also speaking to white

people as a group.

5. Make Inferences

Reread lines 30–35. Circle sentences that give you clues to the speaker's message. Write his message in your own words.

Possible response:

Both races are part of

being American, but

the two groups don't

always like that.

The Savoy Ballroom was an exciting dance spot in Harlem, New York, from the 1920s to the 1950s.

I feel and see and hear, Harlem, I hear you:

hear you, hear me — we two — you, me, talk on this page.

20 (I hear New York, too.) Me — who?

Well, I like to eat, sleep, drink, and be in love.

I like to work, read, learn, and understand life.

I like a pipe for a Christmas present,

or records — Bessie, bop, or Bach.

25 I guess being colored doesn't make me *not* like

the same things other folks like who are other races.

So will my page be colored that I write?

Being me, it will not be white.

But it will be

30 a part of you, instructor.

You are white —

yet a part of me, as I am a part of you.

That's American.

Sometimes perhaps you don't want to be a part of me.

35 Nor do I often want to be a part of you.

Key Vocabulary
understand *v.,* to know the meaning of something well

Musical Background
Bessie is Bessie Smith, an American jazz singer of the 1920s and '30s. *Bop,* also called bebop, is a form of jazz that started in the 1940s. Johann Sebastian *Bach* was a composer of classical music.

But we are, that's true!
As I learn from you,
I guess you learn from me —
although you're older — and white —
40 and somewhat more free.

This is my page for English B. ❖

6. Poetry
Reread lines 36–40. How does the poet use everyday language and grammar in his poem?

Hughes uses phrases

such as "I guess." He

ends the poem very

simply as if he is saying

"The end." He also

uses dashes for pauses

as if he were casually

speaking to someone in

person.

7. Interpret
Why do you think Hughes wrote this poem? What does he want readers to realize? Use the word **realize** in your answer.

He wants readers

to realize how great

the differences are

between the two races

and what it is like to

be the only African

American in his class.

He also wants the

reader to realize that

both races make up

America and what

America is.

Selection Review Theme for English B

A. Answer the questions.

1. Why is it important to make inferences when reading poetry?

Possible response: Poetry consists of words or short phrases that help the reader create images. The reader has to make inferences to understand what the speaker is saying.

2. What inferences did you make while reading "Theme for English B"?

Possible response: When the speaker says that the white instructor has more freedom, I inferred that the poet had experienced discrimination and did not feel he had the same choices as others.

B. Answer the questions.

1. Why is the musical quality of poetry important? How did the rhythm and the sounds of the words help you understand this poem?

Possible response: The musical quality of poetry is important because it is one way you can distinguish poetry from prose. The rhythm created a pattern that made the speaker's words easy to follow.

2. Why do you think the writer chose a poem to express what he had to say?

Possible response: The poem allowed the writer to say or suggest things creatively. He questions himself and this helps the reader see what America is through the speaker's eyes.

3. Do you think the speaker found or created himself? Use details from the poem to support your opinion.

Students should support their opinion with details from the poem.

Reflect and Assess

WRITING: Write About Literature

A. Plan your writing. Read the opinion statement below. Decide if you agree or disagree. List examples from both selections to support your choice. *Answers will vary.*

Opinion: The people and things around us have a big impact on who we are.

I Go Along	Theme for English B

B. What is your opinion? Write an opinion statement. Remember to use the text evidence you listed in the chart to support your opinion.

Students should support their answers with examples from both selections.

_____

_____

_____

_____

_____

_____

_____

_____

Integrate the Language Arts

LITERARY ANALYSIS: Analyze Style

An author uses language in a way that creates a particular **style** and has a certain effect on readers. The techniques authors use to create style include repeating words or phrases, using a combination of long and short sentences, or using incomplete sentences.

A. Read the passage from "I Go Along" below. Look for techniques the author uses to create a style. Then complete the chart.

> First of all, he's only in his twenties. Not even a beard, and he's not dressed like a poet. In fact, he's dressed like me: Levi's and Levi's jacket. Big heavy-duty belt buckle. Boots, even. A tall guy, about a hundred and eighty pounds. It's weird, like there could be poets around and you wouldn't realize they were there.

Style Technique	Example
Repeated words	*even, not, Levi's, like*
Short sentences	"First of all, he's only in his twenties."
Incomplete sentences	"Big heavy-duty belt buckle."
Word choice	*First of all*, *heavy-duty*, *weird*

C. Write a short paragraph explaining how this author's style affects you as a reader.

Answers will vary.

_____

_____

_____

_____

_____

_____

VOCABULARY STUDY: Latin and Greek Roots

Knowing **Latin and Greek roots** and what they mean can help you learn more words in English. For example, you learned that *audience* comes from the Latin root *aud* and means "to hear." The word *program* comes from the Greek root *gram* and means "letter" or "written." *Answers will vary. Possible responses are shown.*

A. Find the root in each word, guess its meaning, and then confirm its definition using a dictionary.

Word	What I Think It Means	Definition
audiotape	a recording	a sound recording on tape
auditorium	a large place where audiences listen to music	a hall used for lectures, concerts, and other events
cardiogram	written record of something	record of heartbeats
telegram	written message from far away	a message sent by telegraph

B. The charts below show some common roots and their meanings. Complete the chart by listing words you've heard that contain each root.

Greek Root	Meaning	Words I've Used
cyclo	circular, wheel	cyclone, bicycle
micro	small	microphone, microscope

Latin Root	Meaning	Words I've Used
dict	hear	dictate, dictionary, diction
port	carry	transport, airport, portable

C. Use the charts above to write a definition of each of these words.

cycle _____ a sequence of events that is repeated over and over again _____

microscope _____ a tool used to see small things _____

dictate _____ to speak so words can be written _____

portable _____ something that can be moved easily from place to place _____

Prepare to Read

▶ **The Pale Mare**
▶ **Caged Bird**

Key Vocabulary

A. How well do you know these words? Circle a rating for each word. Check your understanding of each word's meaning by circling *yes* or *no*. Then write a definition in your own words. If you are unsure of a word's meaning, refer to the Vocabulary Glossary, page 764, in your student text.

Rating Scale

1	I have never seen this word before.
2	I am not sure of the word's meaning.
3	I know this word and can teach the word's meaning to someone else.

Key Word	Check Your Understanding	Deepen Your Understanding
1 claim (klām) *verb* **Rating:** 1 2 3	When you win the lottery, you should **claim** the prize money. (**Yes**)　　No	My definition: *Answers will vary.*
2 freedom (frē-dum) *noun* **Rating:** 1 2 3	In the United States, people do not have any **freedom**. Yes　　(**No**)	My definition: *Answers will vary.*
3 goal (gōl) *noun* **Rating:** 1 2 3	Every new year, many people set a **goal** for what they want to accomplish. (**Yes**)　　No	My definition: *Answers will vary.*
4 ideals (ī-dē-ulz) *noun* **Rating:** 1 2 3	Most people agree that lying and cheating are good **ideals** to live by. Yes　　(**No**)	My definition: *Answers will vary.*

Key Word	Check Your Understanding	Deepen Your Understanding
5 **implore** (im-**plor**) *verb* **Rating:** 1 2 3	When you **implore** someone, you beg him or her. (**Yes**) No	My definition: *Answers will vary.*
6 **roots** (**rüts**) *noun* **Rating:** 1 2 3	People who have **roots** have ties to places and people. (**Yes**) No	My definition: *Answers will vary.*
7 **struggle** (**stru**-gul) *verb, noun* **Rating:** 1 2 3	People who **struggle** when dancing find it very easy to move to the music. Yes (**No**)	My definition: *Answers will vary.*
8 **tradition** (tru-**di**-shun) *noun* **Rating:** 1 2 3	In some families it is a **tradition** to watch football after Thanksgiving dinner. (**Yes**) No	My definition: *Answers will vary.*

B. Use one of the Key Vocabulary words to write about something that is important to you as a person.

Answers will vary.

Before Reading The Pale Mare

LITERARY ANALYSIS: Point of View

A **first-person narrator** is the character in the story who tells it in his or her own words. The narrator includes his or her own thoughts or opinions. Readers need to question what the narrator says about other characters and events.

A. Read the passage below. Underline the words and phrases that tell about the narrator's thoughts and feelings. Use these clues to complete the chart.

> **Look Into the Text**
>
> I sigh. My expertise isn't what he needs. Any fool can take orders. It's not complicated to yell "Four chicken burritos, one green sauce, three red, two large Cokes, two medium 7Ups." No, it's not my expertise in serving food that my precious parents want to preserve. It's that damn tradition again, our *familia* thing, the one that leads to *la raza*, the bigger picture of our people, who we are as Latin Americans. At least that's how Papa and Mama see it. But I don't see things just that way. Not anymore.

Narrator's Thoughts and Feelings About Herself	Narrator's Thoughts and Feelings About Her Parents
thinks anyone can do her job	thinks her parents don't care about her expertise on the job
doesn't care about tradition	thinks her parents just want to preserve tradition

B. Answer the question about the narrator's point of view.

How does the narrator feel about her situation? *Possible response:* She thinks her parents don't care how she feels. She does not care about tradition anymore.

READING STRATEGY: Make Inferences

HOW TO MAKE INFERENCES

1. **Read the Text** Look for the way the narrator says things.

2. **Think About Your Own Experience** Use it to make an inference.

3. **Write Your Ideas On a Self-Stick Note** Place it on the text.

4. **Read On** Notice how your ideas about the narrator change.

A. Read the passage. Use the strategies above to make inferences as you read. Answer the questions below.

Look Into the Text

> Each of my strides jars a different, recent memory. Earlier this week at school, my teacher exclaiming over my work in physics, "Excellent work, Consuela. I'll write a letter of recommendation for you. You should really apply to Cal Tech and MIT. You're coming to the weekend astronomy camp, right?" My heart sang. The stars. For the last two years, they are all I've wanted to do: Study them, chart their fierce light, listen to them, learn what they are saying. Stars do talk—really—with radio waves for words. But when I got home from school, an eclipse was on.

1. What changes when Consuela gets home? How do you think her parents feel about her going to camp?

   Possible response: Consuela is happy at school and excited about camp until she gets home and talks to her family.

2. Which of the four strategies did you use to answer question 1? Explain how you used one or more strategies.

   Possible response: I used strategy 1. I noticed that she said, "an eclipse was on" when she got home from school. I also used strategy 2 and made an inference. I have a friend who is not allowed to do certain things because of what her parents believe.

B. Return to the passage above, and circle the words or phrases that helped you answer the first question.

Selection Review The Pale Mare

 Do We Find or Create Our True Selves?
Discover some struggles that people must face about their identity.

A. In "Pale Mare," you found out how people can struggle while trying
to discover who they are. Complete the Story Map with events from
the story.

Story Map:

> **Beginning:**
>
> Consuela argues with her parents about working at the *charreada*.

> **Middle:**
>
> Consuela watches the horses used for the horse-tripping event in the pens. She focuses
>
> on a pale mare that reminds her of her friend, Fai.

> **End:**
>
> Consuela lets the pale mare and the rest of the horses escape from the arena.

1. What is Consuela struggling with?

   Consuela is struggling with her own wishes and the wishes of her parents. She wants to be free, but her

   parents want her to do her duty in the family.

2. Why does Consuela give the horses their freedom? Use **freedom** in
your answer.

   Possible response: Consuela identifies with the horses' situation. She knows how it feels to not have

   freedom.

3. Which event from the story helps Consuela discover who she truly is?

   Possible response: As Consuela frees the horses, she discovers that she truly wants to be free of tradition

   and the restraints of her family.

Connect Across Texts

*In "The Pale Mare," Consuela's **goal** is to have the **freedom** to be who she really is. What does this poem say about freedom?*

CAGED BIRD

by Maya Angelou

A free bird (leaps) *4 beats*
on the back of the wind *6 beats*
and (floats) downstream *4 beats*
till the current ends *5 beats*
5   and (dips) his wing *4 beats*
in the orange sun rays *6 beats*
and (dares) to claim the sky. *6 beats*

Interact with the Text

1. Make Inferences
Circle the words in this stanza that tell about the free bird's actions. What can you infer about it?

Possible response: The bird is free and daring and able to go anywhere it wants. It has a happy existence.

2. Elements of Poetry
Poems have beats that give each line a certain rhythm. Count the beats in each line of the stanza and write the number of beats at the end of each line.

Key Vocabulary
- **goal** *n.*, a purpose
  freedom *n.*, the power to do, say, or be whatever you want
  claim *v.*, to say you have the right to something

In Other Words
current wind

3. Make Inferences

Highlight the words that the poet uses to describe the bird's cage. What can you infer about the cage?

Possible response: The

cage is like a prison

that creates anger and

sadness. I know that

being caged in a place

makes a person angry.

4. Interpret

Underline the words in the fourth stanza that describe the feelings of the caged bird. What causes the bird to feel this way? Why do you think the bird sings?

Possible response:

The bird is locked up.

His wings are clipped,

so he can't fly. It sings

because singing is its

only freedom, and the

only way to express

itself.

But a bird that stalks
down his narrow cage
10 can seldom see through
his bars of rage
his wings are clipped and
his feet are tied
so he opens his throat to sing.

15 The caged bird sings
with a fearful trill
of things unknown
but longed for still
and his tune is heard
20 on the distant hill
for the caged bird
sings of freedom.

The free bird thinks of another breeze
and the trade winds soft through the sighing trees
25 and the fat worms waiting on a dawn-bright lawn
and he names the sky his own.

But a caged bird stands on the grave of dreams
his shadow shouts on a nightmare scream
his wings are clipped and his feet are tied
30 so he opens his throat to sing.

In Other Words
rage anger
trill sound, song
longed for wanted

The caged bird sings
with a fearful trill
of things unknown
but longed for still
35 and his tune is heard
on the distant hill
for the caged bird
sings of freedom.

5. Elements of Poetry

Underline the lines that describe the caged bird's song. What does this symbolize?

Possible response: The bird and song might symbolize racism or injustice. Racism has deprived many of their true freedoms.

6. Make Inferences

What do you think the poet means by "his tune is heard on the distant hill"?

Possible response: The bird's song can be heard because so many people are fighting to be free.

Selection Review Caged Bird

A. The poet uses symbols to represent ideas. Make an inference about each symbol's meaning.

Symbol 1:	**the cage**
Symbol 2:	**the free bird**

1. Inference for Symbol 1: *Possible response:* The cage is a prison that people are in. These cages are physical, emotional, or spiritual.

2. Inference for Symbol 2: *Possible response:* The free bird symbolizes the kind of life that everyone dreams about. Free birds are free to soar through the clouds without a care in the world and are happy.

B. Answer the questions.

1. How do the rhyme and rhythm of the poem make it enjoyable to read?

Possible response: The rhyme and rhythm reminded me of a song. I felt like I was reading to a beat and concentrating on the lyrics.

2. List the two birds' similarities and differences in the Venn Diagram. Then answer the question.

Venn Diagram

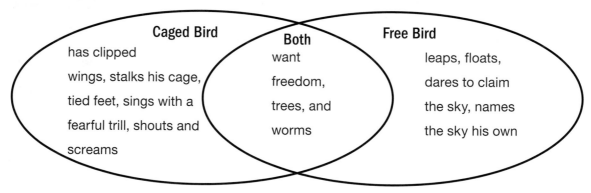

Caged Bird
has clipped wings, stalks his cage, tied feet, sings with a fearful trill, shouts and screams

Both
want freedom, trees, and worms

Free Bird
leaps, floats, dares to claim the sky, names the sky his own

How are the two birds in the poem alike and different?

_____

_____

_____

_____

_____

Reflect and Assess

WRITING: Write About Literature

A. Plan your writing. Write details from each selection that describe the effects of having freedom. *Answers will vary. Possible responses are shown.*

Cause-and-Effect Chart

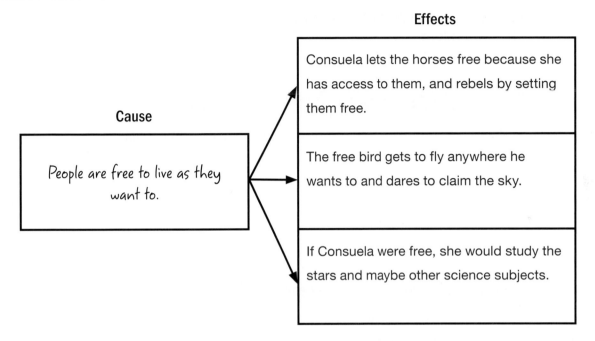

Effects

Cause

People are free to live as they want to.

Consuela lets the horses free because she has access to them, and rebels by setting them free.

The free bird gets to fly anywhere he wants to and dares to claim the sky.

If Consuela were free, she would study the stars and maybe other science subjects.

B. Write a cause-and-effect paragraph explaining what happens when someone has freedom. Support your writing with examples from the selections that you wrote in the chart.

Answers will vary.

Integrate the Language Arts

LITERARY ANALYSIS: Interpret Point of View

Stories can be written from first-person or third-person point of view. Some stories are told from an **omniscient point of view**, by a narrator who is "all knowing." The narrator explains everything that is going on in the story, including each character's thoughts and feelings.

A. Listed below are details you could find out from an omniscient narrator. Write examples of what you might have learned in "The Pale Mare" if it were written from an omniscient point of view.

Details	Examples from "The Pale Mare"
Character's secret thoughts	Mama is worried about Consuela but feels bad for her.
Events the main character doesn't know about	what happens to Consuela after letting the horses free
Things that have happened in the past	the reasons Consuelo's father has for wanting Consuela to stay home
Things that might happen in the future	whether or not Consuela gets to study astronomy
What every character in the story is thinking	Consuela's brother's reaction to how Consuela is treated

B. Rewrite the following sentences from "The Pale Mare" from an omniscient point of view.

1. I didn't know why I was crying, but tears slid down my chin onto my shirt collar.

Possible response: Consuela started crying. Something was upsetting, but she didn't know what.

2. "That's right," I say admiringly. "Don't even look back." I turn and fade away into the night as shouts from security erupt from a nearby barn.

Possible response: Consuela enjoyed seeing the horses run away into the night. It didn't bother her that security found out because the horses were long gone.

C. Write a brief, fictional conversation between you and a friend using omniscient point of view. How does this help you understand another person's feelings?

Answers will vary.

VOCABULARY STUDY: Word Families

Word families are groups of words that are related by meaning. Sometimes, knowing the meaning of one word in a family can help you understand what a related word means. For example, the word *connect* and *connection* are in the same word family. If you know the meaning of *connect*, you can figure out *connection*.

A. Read each word in the chart. Write a word you know that is from the same family. Then write what the related word means. Use a dictionary to check the meaning.

Word	Related Word	Related Word Definition
astronomer	astronomy	the study of the stars and planets
direct	direction	the way someone or something goes or points
ideals	idealistic	to think that things should be good
light	lighten	to make lighter
tradition	traditional	something that is established or customary

B. Think of related words you know from each family and list as many as you can in the chart.

Word	Words I Know
celebrate	celebration, celebrity
precipitate	precipitation
president	presidential
science	scientific, scientist

C. Use each word you listed in the chart above in a sentence. Check your sentences by confirming the meaning of each word in the dictionary.

1. _____

2. _____

3. _____

4. _____

Key Vocabulary Review

A. Read each sentence. Circle the word that best fits into each sentence.

1. When you achieve a difficult (**category** / (**goal**)), you feel proud.

2. It is a ((**tradition**) / **freedom**) in many families to eat turkey on Thanksgiving Day.

3. Many schools offer (**distorted** / (**advanced**)) classes.

4. When you know something well, you (**transform** / (**understand**)) it.

5. A skilled magician relies on (**appearance** / (**illusion**)) to entertain an audience.

6. Wearing a swimsuit at the beach is ((**normal**) / **serious**) behavior.

7. Some people can trace their (**program** / (**roots**)) through many generations.

8. It is exciting when you ((**realize**) / **claim**) what you want to do in the future.

B. Use your own words to write what each Key Vocabulary word means. Then write a synonym for each word. *Answers will vary. Possible responses are shown.*

Key Word	My Definition	Synonym
1. category	a group of items	set
2. depressed	gloomy and sad	unhappy
3. freedom	the right to do what you want	liberty
4. ideals	ideas about how to act or live	beliefs
5. implore	to beg strongly	plead
6. potential	possibility of	ability
7. solution	way to fix a problem	answer
8. transform	to change the appearance or shape of something	change

Unit 3 Key Vocabulary

advanced	• depressed	ideals	poet	roots	• tradition
appearance	• distorted	illusion	• potential	serious	• transform
• category	freedom	implore	program	solution	understand
claim	• goal	• normal	realize	struggle	weight

• Academic Vocabulary

C. Answer the questions using complete sentences. *Answers will vary. Possible responses are shown.*

1. Who is your favorite **poet** and why?

   My favorite poet is Langston Hughes because he writes about things I can identify with.

2. Describe your **appearance**.

   I am tall, dark, and handsome.

3. When is it important to be **serious**?

   It is important to be serious when a friend wants your advice.

4. How might you recognize **distorted** facts?

   If the facts seemed too good to be true or impossible, I might question them.

5. What are some ways to maintain a healthy **weight**?

   You can maintain a healthy weight by exercising and eating fruits and vegetables.

6. Describe the most recent **program** you attended or watched.

   Last week I attended the school play.

7. How would you feel if someone decided to **claim** your belongings as his or her own?

   I would be upset or angry.

8. Which academic subject do you **struggle** with the most?

   I struggle with math the most.

Prepare to Read

▶ Enabling or Disabling?
▶ This I Believe

Key Vocabulary

A. How well do you know these words? Circle a rating for each word. Check your understanding of each word by circling *yes* or *no*. Then write a definition. If you are unsure of a word's meaning, refer to the Vocabulary Glossary, page 764, in your student text.

Rating Scale
1 I have never seen this word before.
2 I am not sure of the word's meaning.
3 I know this word and can teach the word's meaning to someone else.

Key Word	Check Your Understanding	Deepen Your Understanding
1 agony (**a**-gu-nē) *noun* **Rating:** 1 2 3	When people are in **agony,** they smile, laugh, and tell jokes. Yes (No)	My definition: *Answers will vary.*
2 avoid (u-**void**) *verb* **Rating:** 1 2 3	People wear sunscreen and hats to **avoid** sunburn. (Yes) No	My definition: *Answers will vary.*
3 consequence (**kon**-su-kwens) *noun* **Rating:** 1 2 3	A **consequence** of a severe thunderstorm might be fallen power lines and floods. (Yes) No	My definition: *Answers will vary.*
4 dependent (di-**pen**-dunt) *adjective* **Rating:** 1 2 3	Pets are **dependent** on their owners for food and water. (Yes) No	My definition: *Answers will vary.*

Key Word	Check Your Understanding	Deepen Your Understanding
5 **enable** (i-**nā**-bul) *verb* **Rating:** 1 2 3	Airplanes **enable** people to travel quickly from one place to another. **(Yes)** **No**	My definition: _Answers will vary._ _____ _____ _____ _____
6 **relationship** (ri-**lā**-shun-ship) *noun* **Rating:** 1 2 3	Your **relationship** with your friends is the same as your relationship with your family. **Yes** **(No)**	My definition: _Answers will vary._ _____ _____ _____ _____
7 **rescue** (**res**-kyū) *verb* **Rating:** 1 2 3	Sometimes search dogs are used to **rescue** people lost in the wilderness. **(Yes)** **No**	My definition: _Answers will vary._ _____ _____ _____ _____
8 **responsibility** (ri-spon-su-**bi**-lu-tē) *noun* **Rating:** 1 2 3	A **responsibility** is something a person should not do. **Yes** **(No)**	My definition: _Answers will vary._ _____ _____ _____ _____

B. Use one of the Key Vocabulary words to write about a helpful relationship you have had. Why was it helpful?

Answers will vary.
_____
_____

Before Reading Enabling or Disabling?

LITERARY ANALYSIS: Nonfiction Text Features

Text features help you understand information. Titles tell what the text is about. Section heads tell the main idea of an entire section. Each paragraph tells about a single idea. Visuals give more information or explain the text.

A. Read the passage below. Find the nonfiction text features, and write it in the diagram below. Then, write the main idea and details of the paragraph in the diagram.

Look Into the Text

The Enabler

   Jerry had a hectic week, so hectic that he didn't have time to study for Friday's social studies test . . .

   "Ma," he said, "please call me in sick. If I don't get some extra time to study I'm going to flunk."

   So Mom called him in sick on Friday, and he got a C when he took the test on Monday. Jerry gave her a big hug and called her his chief helper. Another description would also fit: his chief enabler. If that sounds like a compliment, it's not.

Main-Idea Diagram

Text Feature: section head "The Enabler"
Main Idea: Jerry's mom is an enabler

Detail: Jerry's mom lied to his school so Jerry would have more time to study for a test.
Detail: Jerry calls his mom his chief helper.

B. How did the text feature help you find the main idea and details?

   Possible response: The section head tells me that the paragraph will be about a person who is an enabler.

   As I read, I look for who the enabler is—Jerry's mom. Then, I look for the details that support this main idea.

READING STRATEGY: Identify Main Ideas

HOW TO UNCOVER MAIN IDEAS IN NONFICTION

1. **Form a Question** Turn the section head into a question.

2. **Make a Web** Write your question in the center.

3. **List Details** Find information to answer your question.

4. **Write a Main Idea Statement** Review the question and the details. The answer to your question is the main idea.

A. Read the passage. Use the strategies above to uncover the main idea. Complete the web with a question and details from the passage. Then answer the questions.

Look Into the Text

Alcoholism—and Beyond

Enabling is a term that's been used for a long time as it relates to alcoholism. The term refers to family and friends who smooth the way for alcoholics so that they never have to face the consequences of their behavior. The term *enabler* has been broadened to include anyone who enables a person to continue with destructive behavior.

Details Web

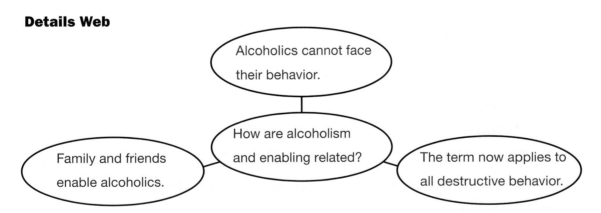

1. Write a main idea statement for this passage.

   Possible response: Alcoholics are often enabled by family and friends, but the term is now used to describe how people enable all destructive behavior.

2. How did the strategies help you find the main idea?

   Possible response: The question in the web helped me find the details that could answer my question.

Selection Review Enabling or Disabling?

How Much Should People Help Each Other?
Read about helpful and harmful relationships.

A. In "Enabling or Disabling?" you read about how people who are trying to help one another can have harmful relationships. Complete the chart with the enablers' behavior and why it is harmful.

Enablers and Their Relationship	What the Enabler Does	Why the Behavior is Harmful
Jerry and his mom	Jerry's mom calls in sick to school for him so he won't flunk his test.	Jerry's mom did not help Jerry. She allowed him to not study for the test.
Jenny and her dad	Jenny pretended her father's drinking was not a problem.	By pretending the problem didn't exist, Jenny was only allowing it to continue.
Janey and Frank	Janey's self-esteem was dependent on the help she gave to Frank.	Janey let Frank's problems become more important than her own life.

B. Use the information in the chart to answer the questions.

1. How were the people discussed in this selection enablers?

   Jerry's mom only helped him make up for not studying. Jenny only allowed her father's behavior to

   continue by not saying anything. Janey let Frank's problems become more important than her own life.

2. Why does an enabler make it their responsibility to fix someone else's problem? Use **responsibility** in your response.

   Possible response: An enabler tries to fix a person in order to feel better. This can make it easy for the

   enabled person to forget that those responsibilities are actually their own.

3. Choose one of the relationships in the chart. How could the individuals turn a harmful relationship into a helpful one?

   Possible response: Janey and Frank could have a healthier relationship if Janey could find ways to make

   herself happy even when Frank is unhappy. This would make her less dependent on him.

Connect Across Texts
You learned about harmful **relationships** *in "Enabling or Disabling?"*
In this essay, Isabel Allende writes about a beautiful relationship.

This I Believe

by Isabel Allende

I have lived my life with passion and in a hurry, trying to accomplish too many things. I never had time to think about my beliefs until my 28-year-old daughter Paula fell ill . . .

Key Vocabulary
relationship *n.*, the way that people are connected to each other

▲ Isabel Allende was a journalist in Chile but left the country in 1975 after her uncle, the president, was killed. Since then, she has written many short stories, articles, and novels.

1. Nonfiction Text Features
Nonfiction selections may be illustrated with photos that tell you what the text is about. Look at the photo and read the caption. How do they help you understand what the text is about?

Possible response:

This photo helps me

understand what the

text is about by showing

one of the important

subjects of this essay.

The caption tells me that

Paula became sick and

died from a rare blood

disease.

2. Interpret
What is the author's attitude toward life despite the death of her daughter? Circle sentences on this page that give you clues.

Possible response: She

has not changed her

values. She still loves life

and believes that helping

others is the only way to

be rich.

She was **in a coma** for a year and I took care of her at home, until she died in my arms in December of 1992.

During that year of **agony** and the following year of **grieving**, everything stopped for me. There was nothing to do—just cry and remember. However, in that experience I discovered there is consistency in my beliefs, my writing and the way I lead my life. I have not changed: I am still the same girl I was fifty years ago, and the same young woman I was in the 1970s. I still lust for life. I am still **ferociously** independent. I still crave justice. And I fall madly in love easily.

Paralyzed and silent in her bed, my daughter Paula taught me a lesson that is now **my mantra**: You only have what you give. It's by spending yourself that you become rich.

Paula was living in Madrid, Spain, when she became sick from a rare blood disease. Allende was by her daughter's side until Paula died.

Paula led a life of service. She worked as a volunteer helping women and children eight hours a day, six days a week. She never had any money, but she needed very little. When she died she had nothing and she needed nothing.

During her illness I had to let go of everything: her laughter, her voice, her grace, her beauty, her company and finally her spirit. When she died I thought I had lost everything. But then I realized I still had the love I had given her. I don't even know if she was able to receive that love. She could not respond in any way—her eyes were **somber** pools that reflected no light. But I was full of love and that love keeps growing, and multiplying, and giving fruit.

Key Vocabulary
agony *n.*, great suffering and worry

In Other Words
in a coma not aware and not moving
grieving being very sad and missing her
ferociously very, extremely
Paralyzed Not able to move
my mantra what I try to do, my motto
somber dark and sad

The pain of losing my child meant I had to **throw overboard all excess baggage** and keep only what is essential. Because of Paula, I don't **cling** to anything anymore. Now I like to give much more than to receive. I am happier when I love than when I am loved. I adore my husband, my son, my grandchildren, my mother, my dog, and frankly I don't know if they even like me. But who cares? Loving them is my joy.

I don't cling to anything anymore.

Give, give, give—what is the point of having experience,

Desperate for a story to tell her sick daughter, Allende wrote a letter that became a best-selling memoir, *Paula*. Allende remembers, "I was not thinking of publishing. My only goal was to survive."

In Other Words
throw overboard all excess baggage
    get rid of things I didn't need
cling hold on tightly

3. Interpret
Do you agree that you can be happier loving your family and friends than feeling loved by them? Why or why not?

Possible response: No.

It would make me feel

uncomfortable if my

friend liked me less than

I liked her.

4. Relate Main Ideas and Supporting Details
Summarize the main idea of this page. Circle and list two details from the text that support it.

Main Idea: Because of

losing her child, Allende

doesn't cling to anything

anymore. Details: Giving

is better than receiving.

She is happier giving

love than receiving it.

5. Interpret

Highlight a sentence that shows the author's viewpoint. Describe the way Allende feels about giving.

Possible response: By giving to others, Allende feels connected to the world and the divine. She feels closer to her daughter.

knowledge or talent if I don't give it away? Of having stories if I don't tell them to others? Of having wealth if I don't share it? I don't intend to be cremated with any of it! It is in giving that I connect with others, with the world, and with the divine.

It is in giving that I feel the spirit of my daughter inside me, like a soft presence. ❖

Selection Review This I Believe

A. Allende wrote a book about her daughter Paula. Read the title and the question, then find the main idea and two details that support it in the essay.

Title: Paula

Question: Why does Allende write about Paula?

1. Detail 1: ___Paula gave her life to community service.___

2. Detail 2: ___Paula had little money and never needed any.___

3. Main Idea: ___Allende wrote about Paula because Paula taught her a lot about giving.___

B. Answer the questions.

1. How did the nonfiction text features (photos and captions) help you understand the essay?

___Possible response:___ The photos reminded me that the essay is about real people, and the captions helped explain why the author wrote the essay.

2. What is something the author learned about people who help others?

___Possible response:___ The author learned that people who help others feel connected to the world and the people around them.

Reflect and Assess

WRITING: Write About Literature

A. What kind of help should parents give their teenagers? Plan your writing.
List evidence from both selections. *Answers will vary.*

How Parents Can Help	How Parents Should Not Help

B. What did you conclude about the kinds of help parents should or should
not give their teenagers? Write a journal entry explaining your beliefs.
Support your beliefs with evidence from both texts.

Students should support their answers with examples from the selections.

_____

_____

_____

_____

_____

_____

_____

_____

_____

Integrate the Language Arts

LITERARY ANALYSIS: Analyze Style

Authors think about their topic, purpose, and audience before writing. Then they choose language that will best express their ideas. This language is the author's **style**.

A. Answer the questions about "This I Believe."

1. What is the topic of the essay?

To give love is better than receiving it. The author learned these lessons from her daughter.

2. Why do you think the author wrote this essay?

Possible response: to persuade; the author wants to honor her daughter by encouraging everyone to

demonstrate love and compassion in their lives.

3. Who might be the intended audience for this essay?

Possible response: I think the audience could be anyone. The author wants to spread her message to as

many people as possible.

B. Read the excerpt from "This I Believe." Find three words or phrases that affect you the most, and list them in the chart. Explain how the author's choice of words makes you feel. *Answers will vary.*

> *I still lust for life. I am still ferociously independent. I still crave justice. And I fall madly in love easily.*

Word or Phrase	How It Makes Me Feel

C. Write a paragraph about someone who has taught you an important lesson. Choose language that will best express your ideas.

Answers will vary.

VOCABULARY STUDY: Multiple-Meaning Words

Many English words have multiple meanings. You can use context clues near an unfamiliar word to figure out the correct meaning of the word.

A. Read the sentences in the chart below. Use context clues to figure out the meaning of each underlined word.

Sentence	Meaning of Underlined Word
I only wear one kind of shoe.	type
The politician made a good pitch for lowering taxes.	argument
Every row in the theater was filled with people.	a line of seats where people can sit
It's my dream to become a movie star.	famous person
You should never park your car next to a fire hydrant.	bring to a stop

B. Write another meaning for each of the underlined words from the chart above. Use a dictionary to confirm each meaning. *Answers will vary. Possible responses are shown.*

kind ___thoughtful and good-hearted___

pitch ___to throw a baseball to the batter___

row ___to use an oar to move a boat___

star ___balls of gas in the solar system that are visible at night___

park ___land set aside for the enjoyment of the public___

C. Each word below has more than one meaning. Write a sentence for each meaning.

match
1. ___*Possible response:* I accidentally went to school wearing socks that did not match.___

2. ___*Possible response:* He lit the campfire with a match.___

turn
1. ___*Possible response:* The child waited impatiently for her turn on the slide.___

2. ___*Possible response:* I was going in the wrong direction, so I had to turn around.___

Prepare to Read

▶ **Brother Ray**
▶ **Power of the Powerless: A Brother's Lesson**

Key Vocabulary

A. How well do you know these words? Circle a rating for each word. Check your understanding for each word by circling *yes* or *no*. Then complete the sentences. If you are unsure of a word's meaning, refer to the Vocabulary Glossary, page 764, in your student text.

	Rating Scale
1	I have never seen this word before.
2	I am not sure of the word's meaning.
3	I know this word and can teach the word's meaning to someone else.

Key Word	Check Your Understanding	Deepen Your Understanding
❶ advice (ud-**vīs**) *noun* **Rating:** 1 2 3	It is sometimes helpful for a person to seek **advice** when making a difficult decision. (**Yes**) No	Good advice I have given is _Possible response: telling_ a friend not to quit school _____
❷ communicate (ku-**myū**-nu-kāt) *verb* **Rating:** 1 2 3	People can **communicate** with each other with their cell phones. (**Yes**) No	My favorite way to communicate is _Possible response: talking on the telephone_ _____
❸ condition (kun-**di**-shun) *noun* **Rating:** 1 2 3	A healthy baby usually has a serious medical **condition**. Yes (**No**)	A medical condition I am familiar with is _Possible response: asthma_ _____
❹ disabilities (dis-u-**bi**-lu-tēz) *noun* **Rating:** 1 2 3	Some people with **disabilities** use special equipment to help them. (**Yes**) No	Two examples of how my school and community support people with disabilities are _Possible response: ramps_ for wheelchairs and sign language interpreters _____

Key Word	Check Your Understanding	Deepen Your Understanding
5 **discipline** (**di**-su-plun) *noun* Rating: 1 2 3	Most parents believe that **discipline** is unhealthy for their children. Yes (No)	An example of effective discipline in school is _____ *Possible response:* lowering a grade for late assignments _____ _____.
6 **hero** (**hear**-ō) *noun* Rating: 1 2 3	A **hero** runs away from danger because he is scared. Yes (No)	Someone I consider to be a hero is ___ *Possible response:* my father _____ _____ _____.
7 **outlook** (**owt**-look) *noun* Rating: 1 2 3	If you are positive, you have a good **outlook** on life. (Yes) No	If I want to change my outlook, I ___ *Possible response:* try to think positively _____ _____ _____.
8 **presence** (**pre**-zuns) *noun* Rating: 1 2 3	To feel someone's **presence**, you have to be in the same room as the person. Yes (No)	I like to be in the presence of ___ *Possible response:* my family and friends _____ _____ _____.

B. Use one of the Key Vocabulary words to tell how you have helped a family member in a special time of need.

Answers will vary. _____

_____

Before Reading Brother Ray

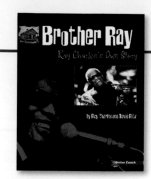

LITERARY ANALYSIS: Text Structure (Chronology)

Authors tell their own life stories in autobiographies. They usually tell about the events in **chronological order**, or the order the events happened.

A. Read the passage below. Find the important events in Ray's life by focusing on time-order words and phrases. Write the events in the Sequence Chain, in the order in which they happened.

> ### Look Into the Text
>
> Mama always wanted me to learn things. Even though she didn't have much education herself, she taught me all she knew—the numbers, the alphabet, the way to spell, how to add and subtract. So when I started going blind, she began to look into schools for me. I was the only blind person in Greenville; people just didn't know what to do with me.
>
> Mama sought out advice. She asked Miss Lad who worked at the post office. She talked to the banker and to Mr. Reams who owned the general store. Soon everyone in town learned about my plight.

Sequence Chain

1. Mama taught Ray the numbers, the alphabet, how to spell, and how to add and subtract.

2. Ray started to go blind.

3. Mama began to look into schools for Ray; she sought out advice.

4. Everyone in town learned about Ray's problem.

B. Complete the sentence.

Everyone in town learned about Ray's blindness after ___his mother asked people she knew for advice about Ray___ .

READING STRATEGY: Summarize Nonfiction

HOW TO SUMMARIZE NONFICTION

1. **Identify the Topic** Look for key words. What is the paragraph mostly about?

2. **Find the Important Information** What is the most important idea?

3. **Summarize the Paragraph** Use your own words to tell about the topic and important information.

A. Read the passage. Use the strategies above to summarize. Answer the questions below.

Look Into the Text

Mama was a country woman with a whole lot of common sense. She understood what most of our neighbors didn't—that I shouldn't grow dependent on anyone except myself. "One of these days I ain't gonna be here," she kept hammering inside my head. Meanwhile, she had me scrub floors, chop wood, wash clothes, and play outside like all the other kids. She made sure I could wash and dress myself. And her discipline didn't stop just 'cause I was blind. She wasn't about to let me get away with any foolishness.

1. What was Mama's attitude toward raising a blind child?

   Mama thought Ray should be treated just like everyone else. She wanted Ray to learn how to take care of

   himself and not expect special treatment just because he was blind.

2. In your own words, what is the most important idea?

   Possible response: Mama felt that Ray needed to do things for himself and to be treated like everyone else.

3. Which of the three strategies did you use to answer question 1?

   Possible response: I used the first strategy. I looked for key words that summarized Mama's attitude toward

   her son.

B. Return to the passage above and circle the words or sentences that gave you the answer to the first question.

Selection Review Brother Ray

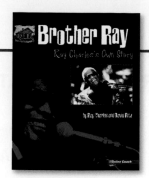

 How Much Should People Help Each Other?
Learn what families do for each other in special situations.

A. In "Brother Ray," you learned how Mama helped Ray the most by encouraging his independence. In the map, list three things that Ray did to be independent. Then write the outcome of his actions.

Goal-and-Outcome Map

> **Goal:**
> Mama wanted Ray to be independent.

↓

> **Action 1:**
> Ray scrubbed floors, chopped wood, washed clothes, and played outside like the other kids.

↓

> **Action 2:**
> Ray learned how to ride a bike on his own and went to a school for the blind.

↓

> **Action 3:**
> After Mama died, Ray listened to Ma Beck's advice about remembering what his Mama told him.

↓

> **Outcome:**
> Ray learned to have faith in himself.

B. Use the information in the map to answer the questions.

1. Why did Mama feel it was so important to make Ray independent?

Mama wanted the best for Ray. She knew that Ray would have to have faith in himself in order to do the things he wanted to do.

2. How did Mama help Ray with his disability? Use **disability** in your answer.

Possible response: Mama helped Ray with his disability by teaching him how to be independent.

Mama sent Ray to a school for the blind, where he learned how to live with his disability.

3. Why might it have been hard for Mama to do the things she did?

Possible response: Ray was her son, and she loved him very much. Sending Ray to school and treating him like a normal child must have been difficult for her as a mother.

Power of the Powerless: A Brother's Lesson

by Christopher de Vinck

Connect Across Texts

In "Brother Ray," Ray Charles tells what happened when he became blind. In this memoir, de Vinck tells about a boy with many **disabilities**.

I grew up in the house where my brother was on his back in his bed for almost 33 years, in the same corner of his room, under the same window, beside the same yellow walls. Oliver was blind, **mute**. His legs were twisted. He didn't have the strength to lift his head nor the intelligence to learn anything.

Today I am an English teacher, and each time I introduce my class to the play about **Helen Keller**, "The Miracle Worker," I tell my students about Oliver. One day, during my first year teaching, a boy in the last row raised his hand and said, "Oh, Mr. de Vinck. You mean he was **a vegetable**."

I **stammered** for a few seconds. My family and I fed Oliver. We changed his diapers, hung his clothes and bed linen on the basement line in winter, and spread them out white and clean on the lawn in the summer. I always liked to watch the grasshoppers jump on the pillowcases.

We bathed Oliver. Tickled his chest to make him laugh. Sometimes we left the radio on in his room. We pulled the shade down over his bed in the morning to keep the sun from burning his tender skin. We listened to him laugh as we watched television downstairs.

Key Vocabulary

disabilities *n.*, problems that can limit what a person does

In Other Words

mute not able to speak
Helen Keller a famous blind and deaf woman
a vegetable someone who can't move or talk (slang)
stammered was not able to speak clearly

Interact with the Text

1. Summarize Nonfiction
Highlight the important information the author tells you about Oliver and his family. Write a sentence that summarizes this relationship.

Possible response:

Because Oliver was confined to bed for 33 years, the author and his family took special care of him.

We listened to him rock his arms up and down to make the bed squeak. We listened to him cough in the middle of the night.

"Well, I guess you could call him a vegetable. I called him Oliver, my brother. You would have liked him."

One October day in 1946, when my mother was pregnant with Oliver, her second son, she **was overcome by fumes** from a leaking coal-burning stove. My oldest brother was sleeping in his crib, which was quite high off the ground so the gas didn't affect him. My father pulled them outside, where my mother **revived** quickly.

On April 20, 1947, Oliver was born. A healthy looking, plump, beautiful boy. One afternoon, a few months later, my mother brought Oliver to a window. She held him there in the sun, the bright good sun, and there Oliver looked and looked directly into the sunlight, which was the first moment my mother realized that Oliver was blind. My parents, the true **heroes** of this story, learned, with the passing months, that blindness was only part of the problem. So they brought Oliver to Mt. Sinai Hospital in New York for tests to determine the extent of his **condition**.

The doctor said that he wanted to make it very clear to both my mother and father that there was absolutely nothing that could be done for Oliver. He didn't want my parents to **grasp at false hope**.

> ## I called him Oliver, my brother. You would have liked him.

Key Vocabulary

hero *n.*, someone whom others admire; someone who acts with courage to help others

condition *n.*, a problem with a person's health

In Other Words

was overcome by fumes lost consciousness because of the strong gas

revived woke up and felt better

grasp at false hope hope for something that would not happen

▲ **Critical Viewing: Character** How do you think the mother in this painting feels about her child? Explain how this relates to Oliver's mother.

"You could place him in an institution," he said. "But," my parents replied, "he is our son. We will take Oliver home of course." The good doctor answered, "Then take him home and love him."

Underline the words that show how the author's parents felt about Oliver after finding out about his disabilities. How do you think their outlook influenced their decision? Use **outlook** in your answer.

Possible response:

Oliver's parents' outlook

influenced their decision

because he was their

son. They cared for him

and wanted the best for

him.

5. Text Structure (Chronology)

Highlight time-order words and phrases that show that the author shifts back to the present. Why does the author do this?

Possible response: The author wants the reader to know that Oliver continues to influence him today.

⚠ **Critical Viewing: Design** Notice the colors and patterns in this painting. How do they make you feel? How does that feeling compare with the feeling of Oliver's home?

Oliver grew to the size of a 10-year-old. He had a big chest, a large head. His hands and feet were those of a 5-year-old, small and soft. We'd wrap a box of baby cereal for him at Christmas and place it under the tree; pat his head with a damp cloth in the middle of a July heat wave. His baptismal certificate hung on the wall above his head. A bishop came to the house and **confirmed** him.

Even now, years after his death from pneumonia on March 12, 1980, Oliver still remains the weakest, most helpless human being I ever met, and yet he was one of the most powerful human beings

In Other Words
confirmed performed a religious ceremony for

I ever met. He could do absolutely nothing except breathe, sleep, eat, and yet he was responsible for action, love, courage, insight. When I was small my mother would say, "Isn't it wonderful that you can see?" And once she said, "When you go to heaven, Oliver will run to you, **embrace** you, and the first thing he will say is 'Thank you.'" I remember, too, my mother explaining to me that we were blessed with Oliver in ways that were not clear to her at first.

So often parents are faced with a child who is severely retarded, but who is also **hyperactive**, demanding or wild, who needs constant care. So many people have little choice but to place their child in an institution. We were fortunate that Oliver didn't need us to be in his room all day. He never knew what his condition was. We were blessed with his **presence**, a true presence of peace.

When I was in my early 20s I met a girl and fell in love. After a few months I brought her home to meet my family. When my mother went to the kitchen to prepare dinner, I asked the girl, "Would you like to see Oliver?" for I had told her about my brother. "No," she answered.

Soon after, I met Roe, a lovely girl. She asked me the names of my brothers and sisters. She loved children. I thought she was wonderful. I brought her home after a few months to meet my family. Soon it was time for me to feed Oliver. I remember **sheepishly asking** Roe if she'd like to see him. "Sure," she said.

> We were blessed with his presence, a true presence of peace.

Key Vocabulary
presence *n.*, the fact or feeling that someone is there

In Other Words
embrace hug
hyperactive overly active
sheepishly asking feeling unsure as I asked

Interact with the Text

6. Summarize Nonfiction
Circle the information that shows what this paragraph is mostly about. Summarize the information in your own words.

Possible response: The family is grateful for having Oliver in their lives and also grateful that he did not seem to be suffering.

7. Interpret

What does the phrase, "power of the powerless" mean in the second paragraph?

Possible response:

Though Oliver is

physically powerless,

he still can bring out a

person's true qualities.

The narrator knew

he would marry Roe

because of the way she

treated Oliver.

I sat at Oliver's bedside as Roe watched over my shoulder. I gave him his first spoonful, his second. "Can I do that?" Roe asked with ease, with freedom, with compassion, so I gave her the bowl and she fed Oliver one spoonful at a time.

The power of the powerless. Which girl would you marry? Today Roe and I have three children. ❖

Key Vocabulary

advice *n.*, ideas about how to solve a problem; suggestions

Selection Review Power of the Powerless: A Brother's Lesson

A. Choose one important event from the story. Summarize the event in two or three sentences.

| Event 1: | Oliver's effect on his family |
| Event 2: | Roe's experience meeting Oliver |

Event: *Possible response:* 1

Summary: *Possible response for Event 1:* Oliver helped his family realize the value of every life. Even though Oliver had special needs, he was capable of loving and being loved.

B. Answer the questions.

1. How did recognizing time-order words help you understand the chronology of the story?

Possible response: The time-order words helped me understand that the author did not want to tell the story exactly in order. He shifted back and forth between past and present.

2. What advice could the author give to parents who have children with disabilities?

Possible response: Believe that they have much to give you, just as you have much to give them.

Reflect and Assess

▶ Brother Ray
▶ Hard Times
▶ Power of the Powerless: A Brother's Lesson

WRITING: Write About Literature

A. What did Ray Charles's and Christopher de Vinck's mothers teach them? List examples in the chart. *Answers will vary.*

Ray Charles's Mother	Christopher de Vinck's Mother
She insisted that Ray get an education and learn to be independent.	She showed loyalty by refusing to put Oliver in an institution.

B. Write a paragraph that summarizes what Ray Charles's and Christopher de Vinck's mothers taught their sons. Support your summary with examples from both selections.

Students should support their answers with examples from both selections.

_____

_____

_____

_____

_____

_____

_____

_____

_____

LITERARY ANALYSIS: Compare Literature and Film

Novels and short stories have inspired many popular films. Filmmakers
sometimes make movies based on nonfiction texts, too.   *Answers will vary.*

A. Read the excerpt from "Brother Ray." Imagine you saw this same scene
in the film version of Ray Charles's story.

> Take my bicycle. Somehow—I can't remember the exact circumstances—I
> was given one. Couldn't have been much older than ten or eleven. Riding was
> something I learned to do quickly. I loved the feeling of motion, and being blind
> wasn't gonna stop me from enjoying the bike.
>
> Now most mamas would die rather than let a blind child scoot around on a
> bike. . . . She let me stray, little by little, further and further away from her. And
> once she saw I was capable of maneuvering this bike, she became less afraid.

Describe how this scene might be different in the film version.

_____

_____

_____

_____

B. Answer the questions about the film version of the same scene.

1. Do you think the film version would include everything from the
excerpt? Explain.

_____

_____

2. How would your feelings about the scene change if you heard
background music?

_____

_____

C. Think of a book or a short story you have read. Describe a scene from
the story. How would your feelings about the events change if you saw a
film version?

_____

_____

_____

_____

VOCABULARY STUDY: Context Clues

When you don't know what a word means, you can look for **context clues** in nearby words and sentences to figure out the meaning. *Answers will vary. Possible responses are shown.*

A. Read the sentences from "Brother Ray." Then write what you think the underlined words mean in each sentence.

Sentence	What I Think the Word Means
She wasn't about to let me get away with any foolishness.	silly behavior
Somehow—I can't remember the exact circumstances—I was given one. Couldn't have been much older than ten or eleven.	way it happened
Folks started worrying about me. No one knew what to do.	people

B. What context clues did you use to figure out the meanings of the words in the chart above?

1. foolishness ___let me get away with___

2. circumstances ___couldn't have been much older than___

3. folks ___started worrying; no one knew___

C. Write a sentence for each of the words above. *Answers will vary.*

1. _____

_____

2. _____

_____

3. _____

_____

Prepare to Read

▶ He Was No Bum
▶ miss rosie

Key Vocabulary

A. How well do you know these words? Circle a rating for each word. Check your understanding of each word by circling the synonym. Then complete the sentences. If you are unsure of a word's meaning, refer to the Vocabulary Glossary, page 764, in your student text.

Rating Scale	
1	I have never seen this word before.
2	I am not sure of the word's meaning.
3	I know this word and can teach the word's meaning to someone else.

Key Word	Check Your Understanding	Deepen Your Understanding
❶ arrange (u-**rānj**) *verb* **Rating:** 1 2 3	To **arrange** something is to _____ it. ignore (organize)	I like to arrange *Possible response:* parties for my family _____ _____ _____ .
❷ destruction (di-**struk**-shun) *noun* **Rating:** 1 2 3	If you see **destruction**, you see _____ . (wreckage) creation	Examples of destruction from a tornado are _____ *Possible responses:* damaged buildings and bridges _____ _____ _____ .
❸ dignity (**dig**-nu-tē) *noun* **Rating:** 1 2 3	If you have **dignity**, you have _____ . anxiety (self-respect)	A situation when you should act with dignity is _____ *Possible response:* at a funeral _____ _____ _____ .
❹ guardian (**gar**-dē-un) *noun* **Rating:** 1 2 3	A **guardian** is a _____ . (protector) competitor	Having a guardian is important when _____ *Possible response:* you are a child _____ _____ _____ .

Key Word	Check Your Understanding	Deepen Your Understanding
5 intervene (in-tur-**vēn**) *verb* **Rating:** 1 2 3	To **intervene** is to get _____. (involved) overlooked	A reason to intervene in a friend's life is _____ *Possible response:* if he or she is in trouble _____ _____ _____.
6 survive (sur-**vīv**) *verb* **Rating:** 1 2 3	To **survive** a disaster is to _____. (live) die	When you survive a difficult experience, you _____ *Possible response:* become stronger _____ _____ _____.
7 veteran (**ve**-tu-run) *noun* **Rating:** 1 2 3	To be a war **veteran** is to be _____. an ex-volunteer (an ex-soldier)	This country can honor a war veteran by _____ *Possible response:* giving him or her a medal _____ _____ _____.
8 willingly (**wi**-ling-lē) *adverb* **Rating:** 1 2 3	If you respond **willingly**, you act _____. gracefully (readily)	Something I do willingly is *Possible response:* help my dad work on his car _____ _____ _____.

B. Use one of the Key Vocabulary words to write about a time you helped
someone who could barely survive on their own.

Answers will vary.

_____

_____

Before Reading He Was No Bum

LITERARY ANALYSIS: Text Structure and Author's Purpose

The **author's purpose** in writing a eulogy is to honor the memory of a person who has died by writing about the person's life. The author usually tells about events in time order, or **chronological order**.

A. Read the passage below. Find the events in Arthur Joseph Kelly's life, and plot them in the Sequence Chain.

> **Look Into the Text**
>
> A bum died. That's what it seemed like. They found his body in a flophouse on West Madison Street, Chicago's Skid Row. White male, approximately fifty-five years old. A bum died.
>
> They didn't know.
>
> He was no bum. And his story . . . well, let his story tell itself.
>
> The man's name was Arthur Joseph Kelly. Growing up, he wanted to be a firefighter. When he was a child he would go to the firehouse at Aberdeen and Washington, the home of Engine 34. His two sisters would go with him sometimes. The firefighters were nice to the kids. This was back in the days when the neighborhood was all right.

Sequence Chain

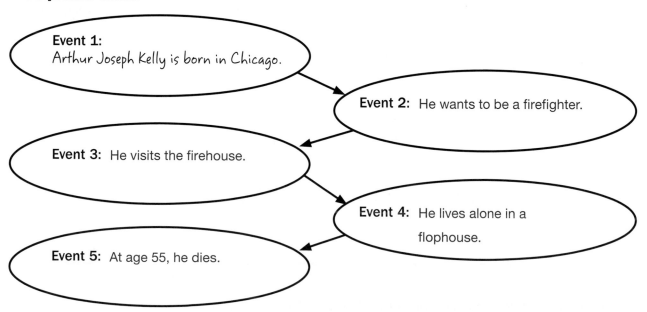

Event 1: Arthur Joseph Kelly is born in Chicago.

Event 2: He wants to be a firefighter.

Event 3: He visits the firehouse.

Event 4: He lives alone in a flophouse.

Event 5: At age 55, he dies.

B. Answer the question about Arthur Joseph Kelly.

How does the author honor Arthur Joseph Kelly? _Possible response:_ The author writes about Kelly's life in chronological order. He describes Kelly as more than a "bum."

READING STRATEGY: Determine What's Important to You

HOW TO DETERMINE WHAT'S IMPORTANT TO YOU

1. **Identify the Topic** Note what the author is talking about.

2. **Find Important Details** Choose key details about the topic.

3. **Focus on Relevant Details** Find details that remind you of someone or something in your life.

A. Read the passage. Use the strategies above to determine what's important to you as you read. Answer the questions below.

> **Look Into the Text**
>
> Arthur Joseph Kelly became a teenager, and then a man, and he never quite had what it takes to be a firefighter. He didn't make it. He did make it into the Army. He was a private in World War II, serving in the European Theater of Operations. He didn't make out too well. He suffered from shell shock. It messed him up pretty badly.
>
> He was placed in a series of military hospitals, and then, when the war was over, in veterans' hospitals. Whatever had happened to him in the service wasn't getting any better.

1. What event changed Kelly's life?

   He joined the Army and fought in World War II. He suffered from shell shock.

2. Underline the detail in the passage above that is most relevant to you. Explain why the detail is relevant to you and how it might help you understand this person's life.

   Possible response: I know someone who has suffered from being in a war. I think I will be able to

   understand Kelly's experience better.

B. Circle the words or sentences in the passage above that give important details about Kelly.

Selection Review He Was No Bum

EQ **How Much Should People Help Each Other?**
Read about people who can barely survive on their own.

A. In "He Was No Bum," you found out how a group of firefighters helped a veteran in need. Write details about how they helped Kelly in the Details Web below.

Details Web

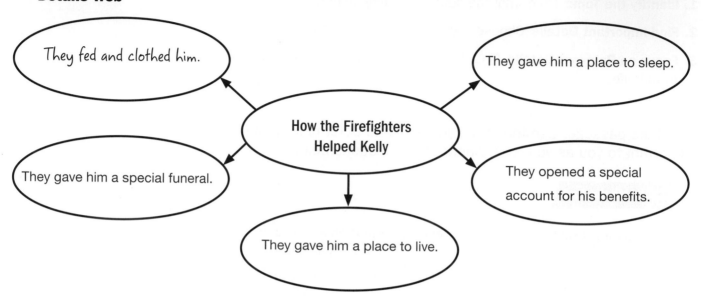

They fed and clothed him.

They gave him a place to sleep.

How the Firefighters Helped Kelly

They gave him a special funeral.

They opened a special account for his benefits.

They gave him a place to live.

B. Use the information in the Details Web to answer the questions.

1. What is the most important thing the firefighters did to help Kelly? Explain why you think so.

   Possible response: They helped Kelly by opening a special account for his money. This might have helped him the most by allowing him to survive with some money of his own.

2. How did the firefighters help Kelly to survive? Use **survive** in your answer.

   Possible response: Kelly was having trouble adjusting to life after the war. The firefighters gave him a place to live, fed him, and helped him manage his veterans' benefits. The firefighters helped him survive.

3. A eulogy honors the memory of a person who has died. What do you think is the most important thing people should remember about Kelly?

   Possible response: He was a good person. He wanted to help others by being a firefighter, but instead he helped to defend our country by becoming a soldier.

Connect Across Texts
In "He Was No Bum," firefighters **intervened** to help Arthur Joseph Kelly **survive**. Who helps a needy woman in this poem?

miss rosie
by Lucille Clifton

when i watch you
<u>wrapped up like garbage</u>
sitting, surrounded by the smell
of too old potato peels
5   or
when i watch you
in your old man's shoes
with the little toe cut out
sitting, waiting for your mind
10   like next week's grocery
i say
when i watch you
you wet brown bag of a woman
who used to be the best looking gal in georgia
15   used to be called the Georgia Rose
i stand up
through your destruction
i stand up

Old Woman, 2005, Maia Stefana Oprea. Acrylics, watercolor and ink, private collection of Ortansa Van Der Wateren, London.

▲ **Critical Viewing: Design** Study the lines in this painting. How do they add to the work? Compare the feeling of the art to the feeling of the poem.

Key Vocabulary
- **intervene** *v.*, to get involved
- **survive** *v.*, to live, to last
  destruction *n.*, ruin, wreckage

In Other Words
peels skins
the Georgia Rose a beautiful woman whom everyone loves

Interact with the Text

1. Figurative Language
Underline the simile that tells what Rosie is wrapped up like. What image do you have of Rosie when you read this comparison?

Possible response: I have an image of an old woman wrapped in layers of mismatched, ragged clothing.

Prepare to Read
▶ Jump Away
▶ Showdown with Big Eva

Key Vocabulary

A. How well do you know these words? Circle a rating for each word. Check your understanding of each word by circling *yes* or *no*. Then complete the sentences. If you are unsure of a word's meaning, refer to the Vocabulary Glossary, page 764, in your student text.

Rating Scale	
1	I have never seen this word before.
2	I am not sure of the word's meaning.
3	I know this word and can teach the word's meaning to someone else.

Key Word	Check Your Understanding	Deepen Your Understanding
❶ attitude (**a**-tu-tüd) *noun* **Rating:** 1 2 3	Your **attitude** can affect the way other people perceive you. **(Yes)** No	I have a good attitude about *Possible response:* moving to a new city next year _____ .
❷ bully (**boo**-lē) *noun; verb* **Rating:** 1 2 3	A **bully** is someone who would defend a younger student. Yes **(No)**	A bully makes me feel *Possible response:* angry _____ .
❸ challenge (**cha**-lunj) *verb* **Rating:** 1 2 3	A boxer might **challenge** his opponent to another match. **(Yes)** No	People who challenge me to reach my goals are _____ *Possible response:* my parents and my coach _____ .
❹ confront (kun-**frunt**) *verb* **Rating:** 1 2 3	Parents might **confront** their children if they stay out too late. **(Yes)** No	You should confront friends if *Possible response:* they do something that could hurt themselves or others _____ .

Key Word	Check Your Understanding	Deepen Your Understanding
5 **intimidate** (in-**ti**-mu-dāt) *verb* **Rating:** 1 2 3	High school seniors often **intimidate** freshmen. (**Yes**) No	Some things that intimidate me in my life are_____ *Possible response:* sports, speaking in public _____ _____ _____ .
6 **reform** (ri-**form**) *verb* **Rating:** 1 2 3	When a person makes a mistake, it is impossible to **reform.** Yes (**No**)	A person needs to reform if he or she _Possible_ _response:_ gets involved in illegal activities _____ _____ _____ .
7 **revelation** (re-vu-**lā**-shun) *noun* **Rating:** 1 2 3	A famous philosopher would keep a **revelation** to himself. Yes (**No**)	It was a revelation to me when I found out that _____ *Possible response:* my mom wanted to be a doctor when she was younger _____ _____ .
8 **sympathetic** (sim-pu-**the**-tik) *adjective* **Rating:** 1 2 3	Friends who listen to your problems are **sympathetic.** (**Yes**) No	It's easy for me to be sympathetic to others who_____ *Possible response:* are very sick _____ _____ _____ .

B. Use one of the Key Vocabulary words to tell about an experience you had when someone treated you badly. What did you do?

Answers will vary. _____

_____

Before Reading Jump Away

LITERARY ANALYSIS: Theme

The **topic** is what the story is about, and the **theme** is the author's message about that topic. Authors usually don't tell you the theme, so take notes about the characters' thoughts, words, and actions, as well as the story's ending, for clues about a story's theme.

A. Read the passage below. Write notes about the theme in the chart.

> ### Look Into the Text
>
> Fenny wasn't scared that way. He wasn't bothered by heights. That's not why he was clinging to the bridge railing. He just didn't want to go in before Mike said so. That'd mean certain trouble for him at school. Today was their turn. Six or seven of them, all the oddballs on campus, challenged to jump from Jensen's Bridge to prove themselves to Mike and the rest of his crew of strong-arms.

Type of Clue	Text Clue
Topic	being bullied
Characters' Thoughts, Words, and Actions	*Possible responses:* Fenny is not scared of heights, but he is scared of Mike. Six or seven of the "oddballs" on campus are there. Mike and the other strong-arms are forcing them to jump.

B. Complete the sentence about the paragraph's theme.

The theme of this paragraph could be _Possible response: that bullies can make people do things that they would normally not do_

_____.

READING STRATEGY: Make Connections

HOW TO MAKE CONNECTIONS

1. **Text to Self** Does this detail remind you of your own life? Explain.

2. **Text to Text** Does this detail remind you of another story or text? Explain.

3. **Text to World** Does this detail relate to issues in the world? Explain.

A. Read the passage. Use the strategies above to make connections as you read. Then answer the questions below.

Look Into the Text

. . . Mike glared at him. "I said go on three. My three. Not two, not two and a half. And definitely not your three. That too difficult a plan for you?" See, things hadn't changed much. Mike was still a jerk.

"Easy enough plan. Your three, not mine. You were just taking your sweet time, though. Like you were having a hard time figuring what came after two."

Fenny saw the others tilt their heads up and in his direction. One or two of them leaned up on an elbow. Mike inched his way up to Fenny with his chest sticking out, his slicked-back hair shining in the sun. "What'd you say?" Now the two were up on each other, face to face, breathing heavy.

"I know you just didn't speak out of turn. And I know you didn't just say what I think I heard you say. Right?"

1. If you were Fenny, how would you respond to Mike? Explain.

   Possible response: I would say "Yes, I did." It is important to stand up to a bully like Mike. A bully keeps

   bullying you.

2. Which strategy did you use to answer question 1?

   Possible response: I used the Text to Self strategy. I can relate to Fenny because I was bullied once.

B. Use a different strategy above to make connections. Explain how you used it.

   Possible response: I used the Text to Text strategy. This situation reminds me of the situations in a book I

   read, *Lord of the Flies.*

Selection Review Jump Away

EQ **Do People Get What They Deserve?**
Find out how people deal with bullies.

A. In "Jump Away," you read how Fenny and the others react to being bullied. In the Character Description Map, write what the characters do and what their actions show about them.

Character Description Map

Character	What the Character Does	What This Shows About the Character
Fenny	is bullied into jumping off a bridge but, in the end, jumps on his own time	Fenny has the desire and the ability to stand up to the school bully.
Mike	pressures Fenny and others to jump off a bridge and becomes angry when Fenny jumps on his own time	Mike is a bully and no matter who stands up to him, he will still be a bully.
The "oddballs" from campus	are bullied by Mike into jumping	They are afraid of Mike and will allow themselves to be bullied.

B. Use the information in the map to answer the questions.

1. What is the theme of "Jump Away"? How did making notes about the characters help you figure out the theme?

   Possible response: A bully will not stop being a bully just because someone stands up to him. By making notes about the characters, I was able to see what happened when Fenny stood up to Mike.

2. Do Fenny and his friends deserve to have Mike intimidate them into jumping off the bridge? Explain. Use **intimidate** in your answer.

   Possible response: No. Nobody deserves to have someone intimidate them. Mike thinks he is stronger than Fenny. Fenny feels pressured to show Mike he is not a coward.

3. How would this story have been different if Fenny had decided not to jump? Explain.

   Possible response: The story would probably end the same way, even if Fenny decided not to jump. Mike would think Fenny was a coward and would beat him up anyway.

Connect Across Texts

In "Jump Away," Fenny figures out how he will deal with a threat from Mike. In this personal narrative, a student tells how she dealt with a **bully**.

SHOWDOWN WITH
BIG EVA
by Laila Ali

I saw my sophomore year as a new beginning. I was looking forward to going to a new high school and was happy to be starting out fresh . . .

▲ The author, Laila Ali, became a professional boxer like her famous father, Muhammad Ali.

Key Vocabulary
bully n., a person who is repeatedly mean to others

1. Interpret
Look at the photo on page 161. Make a prediction about how Laila will choose to deal with her bully.

Possible response: I

predict that Laila will

choose to fight with

her bully because the

picture shows a girl

wearing boxing gloves.

2. Make Connections
Circle the words and phrases that show what Laila wanted as she began high school. What does this remind you of? What strategy did you use to figure out the connection?

Possible response: This

reminds me of wanting a

fresh start when I began

high school; Text to Self.

3. Theme
Underline the words and phrases that show what Big Eva and Laila do that could be clues to the theme. What do their words and actions tell you?

Possible response: Big

Eva is a bully who was

provoking a fight, but

Laila did not back down.

She had the courage to

deal with Big Eva.

I even got a new hairdo, a short cut that made me feel more mature. It was a clean look; I was looking for a clean start.

My older sister, Hana, and my best friend, Alice, had been going to Hamilton High, where they seemed to be having fun. I knew there were cliques, but I figured I'd find my own place.

I was at Alice's house a month before school started when I felt the first twinge of trouble. Alice was on the phone with a girl **reputed** to be the roughest sister at Hamilton. For some reason this girl had **attitude** about me and was **talking mess**. She was telling Alice how she had every intention of kicking my butt. "If she's talking about me," I said, "let her say it to me."

I got on the phone.

"I hear you think you're **all that**," said the girl I'll call Big Eva.

"I don't think anything."

"Well, don't think you can just stroll over to Hamilton and be cool. Because you can't. I don't want you there. If you show up that first day, I'll **whup you**."

"Tell you what," I said, "not only will I show up that first day, but I'll personally come over and introduce myself to you. That way you don't have to go looking for me."

"You don't know who you talking to."

"I **ain't** talking to anyone." And with that, I hung the phone up in her ear.

Hana Ali (left), Muhammad Ali, and Laila. This photo was taken many years after Hana and Laila met Big Eva.

Key Vocabulary
- **attitude** *n.*, **1**: a way of feeling about or looking at the world **2**: unfriendly or negative feelings toward someone or something

When the first day of school came around, I was ready. Because Hana had preceded me at Hamilton, no one quite knew what to make of me. Hana was sweet; I was fire. Hana was friendly; I was **reserved**. **I gave off a don't-mess-with-me vibe.** And I wasn't interested in joining any clique. I've always gone my own way. Alice and Hana were my only friends—and that was enough. In fact, I was with Alice and Hana when I had my first "encounter." We were heading toward the school's main entrance.

A group of seven or eight tough-looking girls were hanging out on the steps. They all had attitudes. The biggest among them had a deep cut across her face. I wouldn't call her pretty.

"That's Big Eva," whispered Alice. I had figured as much.

I walked over to Big Eva and stood right in front of her, toe to toe.

"I'm Laila."

I walked over to Big Eva and stood right in front of her...

Big Eva started rolling her neck, chewing gum and scowling like she wanted to fight. I still didn't know why and I didn't care. I wasn't budging.

"I told you I'd introduce myself," I said. "So here I am."

"Girl," she said, "you don't know who you're messing with."

Her girls **closed ranks** and started moving in on me. I still didn't budge. That's when the bell rang.

"After school," said Big Eva. "I'll be looking for you."

"I'll save you the trouble. I'll meet you right here."

Word got out. The whole school was **buzzing with anticipation**.

In Other Words
reserved quiet
I gave off a don't-mess-with-me vibe. People thought that they should stay away from me.
closed ranks stepped close together
buzzing with anticipation excited

4. Make Connections
Underline the words and phrases that describe Laila and Hana. How are they similar to people you have read about or know personally? What strategy did you use to answer?

Possible response: I know people who are friendly like Hana. I also know people who stand up for themselves like Laila; Text to Self.

5. Theme
Highlight the words or phrases that show how Laila solved her problems with Big Eva. Why did Laila act this way? Explain.

Possible response: Laila confronted Big Eva in order to stop Big Eva from bullying her. Laila refused to start the fight but wanted to show Big Eva that she was not afraid.

Underline the details that describe the scene. How do these details help you as you read the narrative? How did you make a connection?

Possible response: I can

picture the scene in my

mind because I have

seen *Grease*, and I eat

at Taco Bell. I made a

connection to myself.

7. Interpret
What is your opinion about how Laila handled the situation at Taco Bell?

Possible response: I

think she handled it

well because she did

not back down. She

still dealt with Eva and

showed courage.

Big Eva, who wouldn't back down, and Laila Ali, who wouldn't be **intimidated**, were going head to head.

When the final bell rang at 3:30, I was back on the steps, waiting for Big Eva, with a crowd gathering round. Everyone wanted action, and I was ready for *whatever*. When Eva didn't show up, I was half-relieved, half-disappointed. I started walking to Taco Bell, and a large group walked with me. After a few steps, I looked across the street and saw Big Eva and her girls, heading for the same place. A large group also trailed them. It was a scene straight out of *Grease*.

> **...I was ready for *whatever*.**

When we got to Taco Bell, I ordered, then found a seat on one side of the restaurant. Eva's gang sat on the other. I wasn't sure what she wanted to do, but I was going to let her make the first move because she was the one who had the problem with me.

Hana, Alice, and I sat there for a good half hour. By then the place was packed with Hamilton students waiting for a **brawl**. I felt a hundred eyes on me, but I just sat and ate my taco. When I was finished, I got up, slowly walked past Eva's table and, without saying a word, dumped my garbage in the trash. Eva kept rolling her neck, but she never made a move. Nothing happened—until the next day.

I was in the girls' room when Big Eva showed up. "**You're all show and no go**," she said.

"Fine," I said. "Let's go."

She shoved me hard. I shoved her back harder. And just as we were about to **get cracking**, a teacher walked through the door. A few seconds later we were sitting in the principal's office.

Key Vocabulary
intimidate *v.*, to make someone feel unimportant or afraid

In Other Words
Grease a musical about teens in the 1950s
brawl fight
You're all show and no go You talk a lot, but you don't do anything
get cracking really start fighting

The principal started a long speech about the **futility** of fighting. I interrupted her.

"Look," I said directly to Big Eva, "I'm not interested in fighting. I never was. I just wasn't about to be **bullied**. What makes you think you can go around here bullying everybody?"

I expected Eva to start talking more mess. Instead, something amazing happened. Big Eva started crying. I mean, big tears. Maybe it was because the door was closed and we were alone in that office; maybe because she'd been holding it in so long; or maybe because she sensed that I wasn't really angry at her. Whatever the reason, in between tears she **let loose** all the reasons she'd been acting the bully. All her tears and fears came spilling out—how she hated being overweight, how she felt ugly inside, how she never got any attention at home, how the only way she beat back bad feelings was by intimidating others, how deep down she really hated herself and the **ugly front she had created** to scare off the world.

I was shocked by Big Eva's gut-honest **revelations**. And also moved—so moved that I shed a few tears myself. I knew she was being honest; I could feel all the hurt this girl had suffered. I even put my arms around her and let her cry in my arms—both of us sobbing. Two girls who twenty minutes earlier were ready to fight were now acting like long-lost sisters. It was crazy, but in its own way, it was beautiful.

Laila uses her fighting spirit in her boxing. In 2002, she won a best female athlete award from Black Entertainment Television.

Key Vocabulary
bully v., to threaten
- **revelation** n., something that is revealed, or made known

In Other Words
futility uselessness
let loose started to talk about
ugly front she had created mean way she acted

Interact with the Text

8. Interpret
Highlight the words and phrases that show how Laila showed support for Big Eva. What do these actions show you about Laila?

Possible response:

Laila showed that she

is a loving and kind

person. She was willing

to forgive someone

who has hurt her, which

shows great maturity.

9. Interpret

Read the events in the time line. Do you think the experience with Big Eva led Laila to her decision to be a professional boxer? Why or why not?

Possible response:

No. Laila seems like

she is a fighter and a

survivor. Her father

may have led her to

this decision.

I'm not saying Big Eva **reformed** and joined the Girl Scouts, but **the chip was off her shoulder**. From that day on, Big Eva and I were cool. ❖

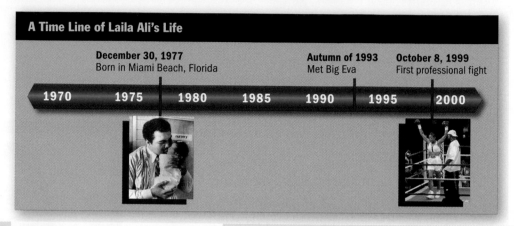

A Time Line of Laila Ali's Life

December 30, 1977
Born in Miami Beach, Florida

Autumn of 1993
Met Big Eva

October 8, 1999
First professional fight

1970   1975   1980   1985   1990   1995   2000

Key Vocabulary
reform *v.*, to change for the better
confront *v.*, to meet someone face-to-face about a problem or to face a difficult situation

In Other Words
the chip was off her shoulder she wasn't so angry anymore

Selection Review   Showdown with Big Eva

A. Make connections to "Showdown with Big Eva" using the three strategies. Write your connections below.

Text to Self:	*Possible response:* when an older student bullied me
Text to Text:	*Possible response:* Mike and Fenny in "Jump Away."
Text to World:	*Possible response:* countries who threaten to go to war

B. Answer the questions.

1. How did knowing how the characters changed help you figure out the theme of the story? What is the theme?

Possible response: I understood why Laila acted confident and why Big Eva acted so tough.

People who bully others are often unhappy and insecure.

2. How would Big Eva and Laila answer the question, "Do people get what they deserve?" Would they answer it differently? Why or why not?

Possible response: Big Eva would say that people don't get what they deserve because she may

feel she deserves more than she gets at home. Laila would say that people do get what they

deserve because Eva got in trouble for being a bully.

Reflect and Assess

WRITING: Write About Literature

A. Plan your writing. The selections present different views of how a bully reacts when confronted. List examples from the selections that show how each bully reacts. *Answers will vary.*

Jump Away	Showdown with Big Eva

B. Which narrative do you think is more realistic in showing how bullies react? Why? Write an opinion statement. Use examples from both texts to support your opinion.

Students should support their answers with examples from both selections.

_____

_____

_____

_____

_____

_____

_____

_____

_____

_____

Integrate the Language Arts

LITERARY ANALYSIS: Analyze Mood and Tone

The **mood** of a story is the feeling you get when you read it. The **tone** is the author's attitude toward the characters and the topic. *Answers will vary.*

A. Read the sentences from "Jump Away." Describe how these sentences make you feel. Then write what you think the author's attitude might be.

Sentence	How It Makes Me Feel	Author's Attitude
"'Any of you girls want to back out?'"		admiring, proud
"'Don't worry about me. I'm jumping. I'm just waiting for the word.'"		carefree, at ease
"Even if he jumped today, he'd still be Femmy at school. Mike would still be the jerk who pushed him around."		nervous, apprehensive

B. Use the information in the chart above to answer the questions.

1. How would you describe the mood of this story? Give examples. _____

_____

2. How would you describe the story's tone? _____

_____

C. Imagine that Fenny's actions do change his relationship with Mike. Write a new ending to the story. Show your feelings and attitude.

_____

_____

_____

_____

_____

_____

_____

_____

VOCABULARY STUDY: Relate Words

One strategy to learn new words is to put them in groups, or categories. For example, the words *intimidate* and *confront* are both related to things that bullies do. *Answers will vary.*

A. Think of words that describe a brave person. Use a thesaurus to find synonyms, or words with similar meanings. List them in the web.

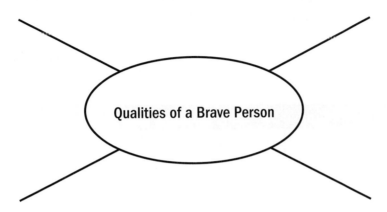

Qualities of a Brave Person

B. Relate the words you wrote in the web to what you know about the meaning of the word *brave*. Write what you think each word means. Use a dictionary to confirm your definitions.

1. _____

2. _____

3. _____

4. _____

C. Write a sentence using each word in your web.

1. _____

_____

2. _____

_____

3. _____

_____

4. _____

_____

Prepare to Read

▶ Fear
▶ Violence Hits Home

Key Vocabulary

A. How well do you know these words? Circle a rating for each word. Check your understanding of each word by marking an *X* next to the correct definition. Then complete the sentences. If you are unsure of a word's meaning, refer to the Vocabulary Glossary, page 764, in your student text.

Rating Scale

1	I have never seen this word before.
2	I am not sure of the word's meaning.
3	I know this word and can teach the word's meaning to someone else.

Key Word	Check Your Understanding	Deepen Your Understanding
❶ defiant (di-**fī**-unt) *adjective* **Rating:** 1 2 3	☒ resistant or challenging ☐ clear and exact	Children are defiant when *Possible response:* they are told they can't have something they want
❷ intruder (in-**trud**-ur) *noun* **Rating:** 1 2 3	☐ an invited guest ☒ an unwelcome visitor	Things people do to protect their homes from an intruder are *Possible response:* keep the doors locked, get a security system
❸ motivate (**mō**-tu-vāt) *verb* **Rating:** 1 2 3	☒ to move toward action ☐ to move away from an object	My friends motivate me to *Possible response:* practice music
❹ positive (**po**-zu-tiv) *adjective* **Rating:** 1 2 3	☒ good or helpful ☐ critical	I expect to have a positive experience when I _____ *Possible response:* hang out with my brothers

Key Word	Check Your Understanding	Deepen Your Understanding
5 **reaction** (rē-**ak**-shun) *noun* **Rating:** 1 2 3	☐ an action that is quick ☒ an action that is a response	When I make a mistake, my reaction is to _____ *Possible response:* try to fix it _____ _____ _____ .
6 **response** (ri-**spons**) *noun* **Rating:** 1 2 3	☒ a reply or an answer ☐ a kind of invitation	When I hear a song I like, my response is to _____ *Possible response:* start singing _____ _____ _____ .
7 **revenge** (ri-**venj**) *noun* **Rating:** 1 2 3	☒ retaliation or payback ☐ discipline or order	An action that might cause someone to seek revenge would be _*Possible response:* spreading lies about a_ close friend _____ _____ .
8 **violence** (**vī**-luns) *noun* **Rating:** 1 2 3	☐ physical exercise ☒ physical force	A possible way to end violence is to _*Possible response:*_ teach people to talk to each other _____ _____ _____ .

B. Use one of the Key Vocabulary words to write about a time you had to respond to a violent situation. What did you do?

Answers will vary. _____

_____

Before Reading Fear

LITERARY ANALYSIS: Theme

Theme is the main message in a story. Look for clues in the title, setting, and the thoughts, actions, and problems of the characters.

A. Read the passage below. Find the clues that will help you determine the theme of the story and write them in the chart.

Look Into the Text

> Alphonso "Zo" Driggers is fourteen years old. He is taller than a lot of kids his age in the neighborhood, taller and thinner. He has lived in the same place since he was born. Two weeks ago, his mother, who lives alone with Zo in their small clapboard house, finally decided to install security bars on the windows and expensive security doors on both the front and back.

Type of Clue	Text Clue
Title	"Fear"
Setting	a small clapboard or wooden house in a neighborhood the characters have lived in for a long time
Actions of characters	Zo's mother installs security bars and doors to protect the house from intruders.

B. Complete the sentence about the theme of the story. Then describe what problem you think the characters will face.

I think the theme of the story "Fear" will be _Possible responses: fear makes people change, or do_ things to protect their families. The characters do not feel safe living in their neighborhoods because Zo's mother installed security bars and doors. I think the characters will have to face an intruder.

READING STRATEGY: Make Connections

HOW TO MAKE CONNECTIONS

1. **Read** with a partner.

2. **Share Ideas** Think about how the story connects to your life, other stories, or the world.

3. **Discuss** Talk to a partner about how your connections help you understand the setting, characters, and plot of the story.

A. Read the passage. Use the strategies above to make connections. Write the details and your connections in the chart.

Look Into the Text

It is a school night, a Tuesday, in early February. Zo's mother, who works as a checker in a grocery store, has an evening shift— something that doesn't happen very often. Zo is home alone. . . . It's a dark night; a winter breeze is blowing along the street outside—not cold, but not warm either. There is a dark feeling to the evening. . . suddenly Zo hears something. . . . Somebody outside is messing with the window in the spare bedroom at the back of the house . . . Zo freezes.

Detail	Connection
Zo is home alone.	Being home alone can be scary.
There is a dark feeling to the evening.	I know that kind of feeling. It's as if you know something bad is about to happen.

1. What do you think Zo is feeling? Explain.

   I think Zo is feeling alone and afraid. The noises in his house are probably scaring him.

2. How does making connections help you understand the character?

   Possible response: I think about how I would react to the same situation. I see how I am similar to or

   different from the characters. I also know that it is scary to be home alone at night.

B. Return to the passage above and circle the words or sentences that gave you the answer to the first question.

Selection Review Fear

 Do People Get What They Deserve?
Find out how people respond to violence in their communities.

A. In "Fear," you found out how a young boy finds the courage to react to violence in his home. Complete the map below.

Problem and Solution Map

> **Problem:**
> Zo is left home alone.

> **Event 1:**
> Zo hears intruders trying to break into the house.
>
> **Event 2:**
> The intruders tell him to open the door, or else.
>
> **Event 3:**
> Zo scares them off by threatening to call the police.

> **Solution:**
> Zo finds enough courage to tell the intruders that he'd rather be dead than afraid of them.

B. Use the information in the Problem and Solution Map to answer the questions.

1. How does Zo find courage to stand up to the intruders?

   He realizes that the intruders are guys from his neighborhood and he cannot be afraid of them.

2. How does Zo frighten the intruders? Use **intruder** in your answer.

   Possible response: Zo threatens to call the police to stop the intruders and acts as though he is the
   one in power.

3. Do you think Zo should have called the police? Why or why not?

   Possible responses: No, I think the intruders will leave Zo and his mom alone now. I think they know that
   Zo will call the police.; Yes, I think Zo should have gotten them in trouble with the police because the
   intruders deserved it.

Violence Hits Home

by Denise Rinaldo

Connect Across Texts

In "Fear," Zo faces **intruders** who are trying to break into his house. In this magazine article, a teen struggles against **violence** in his own community.

A Bad Situation

Growing up in Oakland, California, Antonio Bibb knew about violence. His community **has been plagued by** murders, battles between gangs, and robberies. So when Antonio heard about an anti-violence program for high school students called Teens on Target, he was **intrigued**. He was in the seventh grade at the time, but promised himself that when he got to high school, he'd join the group.

Antonio knew lots of kids who had lost family members to violence. He felt lucky he hadn't, and he wanted to do something **positive**. "I felt like there was no way to stop violence, but I hoped I might be able to change things a bit," Antonio, now 18, says.

He also wanted to show others that he was on the side of peace. "Pretty much every adult on my dad's side of the family has been in jail, including my dad," Antonio says. "Even when I was young, people were starting to judge me and categorize me because of that."

Positive Start

In his freshman year, Antonio joined Teens on Target. By tenth grade, he was doing well in school and had become a leader in the program. He got to travel to Maryland for an anti-violence conference. "It was more than **an extracurricular activity to me**," Antonio says. "I really felt like I was helping to stop younger kids from making the same mistakes adults in their families might be making."

Key Vocabulary

intruder *n.*, someone who goes where he or she should not go

violence *n.*, physical action that is very rough, harmful, and mean

● **positive** *adj.*, good, helpful, favorable

In Other Words

has been plagued by has had many

intrigued very interested

an extracurricular activity to me something I did outside of school

Interact with the Text

1. Make Connections

Circle a phrase that explains how people treated Antonio. Describe a time when you felt that someone judged you before they got to know you.

Possible response: I feel that I have been judged because of the clothes I wear. Some people won't talk to me because I don't wear certain kinds of clothes.

2. Magazine Article

Read the caption on this page. Explain how the photo and caption help you understand Antonio's feelings.

Possible response:

Antonio's serious and

angry look and the quote

help me understand the

turmoil he must have

gone through after his

uncle's death.

3. Interpret

Underline a sentence in the second column that tells how Antonio reacted to his uncle's death. How would responding with revenge change everything he had worked for with Teens on Target?

Possible response: If

Antonio responded with

violence, he would only

be continuing the cycle

of violence in his family.

Antonio stands on the street where his uncle was killed. "I kept thinking of my little cousin growing up without a father," the teen says.

Then, one day during his junior year, Antonio received terrible news. Antonio's Uncle Michael, with whom he had been extremely close, was shot and killed on a street, **in a case of mistaken identity**.

"My father told me and I didn't believe it," Antonio says. "It didn't really **sink in** until I flipped on the news and I saw another one of my uncles on the air talking about it."

Antonio says that he walked through the next several months feeling a combination of disbelief and sadness. His family was **in turmoil**. "They were broken," he says. Sometimes, Antonio had thoughts of **revenge**—of turning to violence himself and **tracking down** his uncle's killer. "I kept thinking of my little cousin growing up without a father," he says.

Key Vocabulary
revenge *n.*, the act of hurting someone who has hurt you

In Other Words
in a case of mistaken identity by a killer who thought the uncle was someone else
sink in seem real
in turmoil upset and confused
tracking down finding

Teen in Turmoil

Experts say Antonio's **reaction** was normal for a teen who has lost a close family member to violence.

"Revenge fantasies are common," says Kenneth J. Doka, a professor of psychology at the College of New Rochelle in New York and an expert in **grief** and dying. "The key, of course, is helping people not act out on those feelings."

Thanks to his work with Teens on Target, Antonio understood that and did not seek revenge. The memory of his uncle, who Antonio says was "a very powerful and positive man," also helped.

In the fall of his senior year, Antonio was starting to feel like his old self. Then, tragedy struck again. "I lost my best friend in a gang-related shooting," he says. Antonio **snapped** back into revenge mode, and this time it was worse.

"I was ready to quit Teens on Target," he says. "I felt like I had to get back at somebody. There was no reason for my uncle and my friend to die, and I was going to do something about it."

After his best friend was killed, Antonio really struggled with thoughts of revenge.

Key Vocabulary
• **reaction** *n.*, what you think or do because of something else

In Other Words
grief deep sadness
snapped went

4. Magazine Article
Read the heading of this section. Explain what you think this section of the article will be about. What other features of a magazine article does this page display?

Possible response: The section head tells me that Antonio experienced a difficult time trying to get over his uncle's death. This page shows easy-to-read columns and a photo with an informative caption.

To the Rescue

Who kept Antonio from **snapping**? A woman named Teresa Shartell. Teresa is the Teens on Target program coordinator with whom Antonio had been working since his freshman year. She was his teacher, counselor, and friend.

"Teresa reminded me that lots of kids we work with were going through the same situation I was, and that now I was in an even better position to **motivate** them," Antonio says. "She said they'd see how I was reacting to my situation and that would really help them out."

Antonio says he "took what Teresa said and **ran with it**. I realized that we're all going to go through pain. It's what you choose to do with it that makes you the person you are."

The teen **threw himself into his work** with Teens on Target with more passion than ever. He also **vowed to serve as an inspiration for** his now-fatherless cousin. "A lot of kids turn to violence because they see it at school and at home; they don't have strong role models," Antonio says. "I'm trying to be that role model for my cousin."

Teresa Shartell (right) helped Antonio channel his anger over losing his uncle and friend into helping others keep the peace.

Key Vocabulary
- **motivate** *v.*, to give reason to, to inspire, to stimulate

In Other Words
snapping doing the wrong thing
ran with it really used it, really applied it
threw himself into his work decided to work intensely
vowed to serve as an inspiration for promised to act the right way to help

Root Causes

WHAT CAUSES VIOLENCE? HOW CAN VIOLENCE BE AVOIDED?

FEAR. If someone is afraid to walk down a street, he or she may carry a weapon for protection. A better idea is to talk to someone like a parent, teacher, or counselor who can help resolve a tense situation peacefully.

STEREOTYPING. Violence can result when people are judged by their looks, dress, or who they hang out with. A better idea is to get to know people before you decide how you feel about them.

BAD ROLE MODELS. If kids grow up surrounded by violence, they're going to **emulate** it. Providing positive role models and teaching kids to act peacefully can prevent future violence.

A Life's Work

Antonio plans to **devote** his life to the fight against violence. That includes making sure as few people as possible have to go through the kind of losses he's experienced. One of his goals is to reduce the number of guns on the street. "If it hadn't been so easy to get guns, I think my uncle would still be living," Antonio says.

Now a high school graduate, Antonio has continued to work with Teens on Target and is shopping around for a college to attend. "My life is pretty blessed right now," he says. "I'm doing

In Other Words
emulate copy
devote dedicate

Interact with the Text

5. Interpret
Underline the idea in the first column on page 178 that caused Antonio to become a better role model. Explain how he can be a better role model now.

Possible response: He has experience dealing positively with violence.

6. Magazine Article
Explain how the text box on this page adds important information to the magazine article. Summarize its main points.

Possible response:
The text box shares information that is not in the article. The text box includes three main causes of violence and what teens can do to avoid violence.

7. Make Connections
Circle phrases that tell you about Antonio's goals. What kind of connection can you make to Antonio's goals?

Possible response: I can make a text-to-world connection. I think more people are needed to fight this problem in our society.

8. Interpret
Underline three phrases or sentences that show some of Antonio's advice. Explain his message in your own words.

Possible response: Don't

follow what everyone

else is doing. It's better

to be yourself.

exactly what I want to do." Antonio is used to giving advice to kids. "Be a leader. Stop following everyone else," he says. "It doesn't matter if you can't buy the stuff you think is cool from movies and videos—**some Phat Farm or some Sean John** or whatever it is. Just be yourself. The more you shine for yourself, the more you can shine in front of everybody else." ❖

In Other Words
some Phat Farm or some Sean John popular clothes or shoes

Selection Review Violence Hits Home

A. Choose one story detail below and make a connection. Identify the connection as Text to Self, Text to Text, or Text to World.

> **Story Detail 1:** Antonio knows at a young age that he wants to work for peace.
> **Story Detail 2:** Antonio chooses to do what is right and does not seek revenge.

Connection: *Possible response:* Zo doesn't fight the intruders in the story "Fear" either; Text to Text

B. Answer the questions.

1. What features of the magazine article helped you understand what the writer was saying?

   Possible response: The subheads helped me focus on the main ideas in each section; the informative captions and photos added interest to the story.

2. If you wrote an email to Antonio, what would you tell him about revenge?

   Possible response: I would let him know that I lost someone and was angry, but talking to other people helped me see that people who commit crimes end up getting punished anyway.

Reflect and Assess

WRITING: Write About Literature

A. Plan your writing. Read the opinion statement below. Decide if you agree or disagree with it. List examples from both selections to support your choice. *Answers will vary.*

Opinion: The government should provide money to groups like Teens on Target.

Fear	Violence Hits Home

B. What is your opinion? Use another sheet of paper and write a letter to the editor of a school or local newspaper. Support your opinion with information from both texts.

Students should support their letters with examples from the selections.

LITERARY ANALYSIS: Analyze Suspense

Suspense is a feeling of uncertainty or excitement about what will happen next. Authors create suspense by putting a character in a dangerous situation, creating a struggle for a character, or having a character face an important decision.

A. Think of examples of how the authors of "Fear" and "Violence Hits Home" create suspense. List your examples in the web.

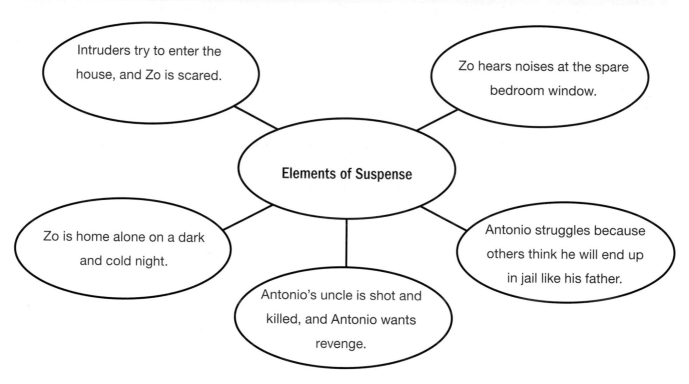

Intruders try to enter the house, and Zo is scared.

Zo hears noises at the spare bedroom window.

Elements of Suspense

Zo is home alone on a dark and cold night.

Antonio struggles because others think he will end up in jail like his father.

Antonio's uncle is shot and killed, and Antonio wants revenge.

B. Answer the questions.

1. How does the author create suspense in "Fear"?

The author creates a dark and scary mood by putting Zo in a situation where he is alone at night. Then the author makes the reader wonder whether or not Zo will be harmed by the intruders.

2. Was the author's technique for creating suspense in "Violence Hits Home" different from the technique used in "Fear"? Explain.

Yes. The suspense was created because the reader was unsure about how Antonio would deal with the death of his uncle and whether or not he would make the right choice.

C. Write a fictional scenario including elements of suspense.

Answers will vary.

VOCABULARY STUDY: Relate Words

Synonyms are words that have a similar meaning. **Antonyms** are words that have opposite meanings.

A. Use a thesaurus to find a synonym and an antonym for each word in the chart below. *Answers will vary. Possible responses are shown.*

Word	Synonym	Antonym
calm	relaxed	excited
inspire	motivate	inhibit
positive	good	bad
powerful	strong	weak
tragedy	disaster	blessing

B. Each set of words below contains two synonyms and one antonym. Underline the antonym in each set.

1. resist, fight, <u>allow</u>

2. fear, <u>calmness</u>, panic

3. powerful, <u>weak</u>, strong

4. good, positive, <u>bad</u>

5. <u>blessing</u>, tragedy, disaster

C. Read each sentence below. Replace each underlined word with a synonym. *Answers will vary. Possible responses are shown.*

1. Antonio wants <u>peace</u> in his community.

harmony

2. The intruders believe Zo's <u>terror</u> will make him open the door.

fear

3. By threatening to call the police, Zo was able to <u>fight</u> the intruders.

resist

4. Antonio's uncle is a <u>strong</u> influence in his life.

powerful

5. Antonio decides that his <u>experience</u> can be a good example for other young people to follow.

ordeal

Prepare to Read

▶ Abuela Invents the Zero
▶ Karate

Key Vocabulary

A. How well do you know these words? Circle a rating for each word. Check your understanding of each word by circling *yes* or *no*. Then complete the sentences. If you are unsure of a word's meaning, refer to the Vocabulary Glossary, page 764, in your student text.

Rating Scale	
1	I have never seen this word before.
2	I am not sure of the word's meaning.
3	I know this word and can teach the word's meaning to someone else.

Key Word	Check Your Understanding	Deepen Your Understanding
❶ assume (u-**süm**) *verb* **Rating:** 1 2 3	You can **assume** a tall person plays basketball. Yes (No)	I assume that the life of a movie star is *Possible* *response:* glamorous and exciting _____ _____ _____ .
❷ compromise (**kom**-pru-mīz) *noun* **Rating:** 1 2 3	A person who makes a **compromise** will not give up. Yes (No)	I made a compromise when *Possible response:* my brothers and I agreed to share the family car _____ _____ _____ .
❸ existence (ig-**zis**-tuns) *noun* **Rating:** 1 2 3	A scientist might think about the **existence** of life on other planets. (Yes) No	An animal that has disappeared from existence is _____ *Possible response:* the dinosaur _____ _____ _____ .
❹ ignore (ig-**nor**) *verb* **Rating:** 1 2 3	A professional football player might **ignore** a minor injury and play through the pain. (Yes) No	I do not want to ignore *Possible response:* my responsibility to my baseball team _____ _____ _____ .

Key Word	Check Your Understanding	Deepen Your Understanding
5 **inconvenient** (in-kun-**vē**-nyunt) *adjective* **Rating:** 1 2 3	An **inconvenient** traffic jam might make you late to a movie. **(Yes)** No	A power outage is inconvenient when _____ *Possible response:* I want to watch my favorite television show _____ _____ _____ .
6 **insult** (in-**sult**) *verb* **Rating:** 1 2 3	Name-calling can **insult** people. **(Yes)** No	I was insulted when *Possible response:* people laughed at my painting _____ _____ _____ _____ .
7 **ridiculous** (ru-**di**-kyu-lus) *adjective* **Rating:** 1 2 3	An elephant might look **ridiculous** wearing a bathing suit. **(Yes)** No	The most ridiculous thing I ever saw was _____ *Possible response:* a dog wearing a hat _____ _____ _____ _____ .
8 **value** (**val**-yū) *verb* **Rating:** 1 2 3	A business owner probably does not **value** his or her customers. Yes **(No)**	The two qualities I value most in a friendship are _____ *Possible response:* trust and loyalty _____ _____ _____ _____ .

B. Use one of the Key Vocabulary words to write about a personal experience where you were insulted. How did you react?

_*Answers will vary.*_____

_____

Before Reading Abuela Invents the Zero

LITERARY ANALYSIS: Theme

The **theme** of a story is its message. These story elements give clues to the story's theme:

- The **title** can indicate the **topic**. The topic gives clues about the theme.
- The **setting** and **plot** help you understand the **characters**.

A. Read the passage below. Look for the clues that tell you about the theme. Then, complete the map.

> **Look Into the Text**
>
> "You made me feel like a zero, like a nothing," she says in Spanish, *un cero, nada.* She is trembling, an angry little old woman lost in a heavy winter coat that belongs to my mother. And I end up being sent to my room, like I was a child, to think about my grandmother's idea of math.
>
> It all began with Abuela coming up from the Island for a visit. It was her first time in the United States. My mother and father paid her way here so that she wouldn't die without seeing snow. If you asked me, and nobody has, the dirty slush in this city is not worth the price of a ticket. But I guess she deserves some kind of award for having had ten kids and survived to tell about it.

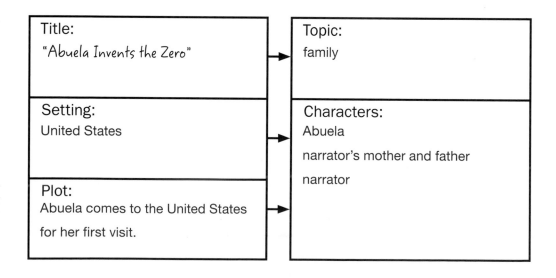

Title:	Topic:
"Abuela Invents the Zero"	family

Setting:	Characters:
United States	Abuela
	narrator's mother and father
	narrator

Plot:	
Abuela comes to the United States for her first visit.	

B. Use the information in the map to complete the sentence.

The theme of this story might be ___*Possible response:* Family loyalty. I think the story will be about___ members of a family who disagree and fight, but who ultimately love each other

READING STRATEGY: Make Connections

HOW TO MAKE CONNECTIONS

1. **Use a Double-Entry Journal** Copy a quote and page number. Write a comment to explain the connection.

2. **Follow Up on Your Comments** As you read more of the story, add new ideas based on what you learn.

A. Read the passage. On a separate piece of paper, write a journal entry using the strategies above. Answer the questions below.

> ### Look Into the Text
>
> So since she's only four feet eleven inches tall, she walks around in my mother's big black coat looking ridiculous. I try to walk far behind them in public so that no one will think we're together. I plan to stay very busy the whole time she's with us so that I won't be asked to take her anywhere, but my plan is ruined when my mother comes down with the flu and Abuela absolutely *has* to attend Sunday mass or her soul will be eternally damned. She's more Catholic than the Pope. My father decides that he should stay home with my mother and that I should escort *la abuela* to church. He tells me this on Saturday night as I'm getting ready to go out to the mall with my friends.
>
> "No way," I say.

1. How does the narrator feel about her grandmother?

   The narrator feels embarrassed by her grandmother. The narrator does not want to be seen with her

   grandmother because of the way her grandmother looks and acts.

2. How did your journal entry help you answer question 1?

   Possible response: My journal entry helped me because I could see both the quote from the passage and

   my ideas about the quote at the same time.

B. Return to the passage above and circle the phrases or sentences that helped you make a connection and answer the first question.

Selection Review Abuela Invents the Zero

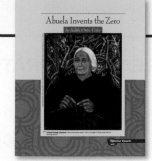

 Do People Get What They Deserve?
Find out what happens to people who insult others.

A. In "Abuela Invents the Zero," you learn how Connie changes after she insults her grandmother. Complete the Flow Chart below.

Flow Chart

> **What she does:**
> Connie ignores her lost grandmother at church. Her grandmother cannot find her way back to her seat.

↓

> **Why she does it:**
> Connie feels embarrassed. Connie worries that people will make fun of her because of how her grandmother looks and acts.

↓

> **What she learns:**
> Connie realizes how her actions affected her grandmother at the church. Connie understands how her grandmother feels.

↓

> **Theme:**
> *Possible response:* It's important to treat family well.

B. Use the information in the chart to answer the questions.

1. How does Connie change from the beginning of the story to the end?

In the beginning of the story, Connie finds her grandmother embarrassing. By the end of the story, Connie understands that her grandmother is a family member who has hurt feelings because of Connie's actions.

2. Why does Connie assume her grandmother is a foolish old woman?
Use **assume** in your answer.

Possible response: Connie assumes that because her grandmother is from a different country, speaks a different language, has different customs, and is much older than Connie, that she is not capable of hurt feelings.

3. How might Connie's relationship with her grandmother change in the future?

Possible response: In the future, Connie might treat her grandmother better. Connie might also be more concerned for her grandmother's feelings and less worried about what her friends think.

Karate
by Huynh Quang Nhuong

Connect Across Texts
In "Abuela Invents the Zero," Connie is unkind to her grandmother. In this personal narrative, find out what happens when someone is unkind to the author's grandfather.

My grandmother had married a man whom she loved with all her heart, but who was totally different from her. My grandfather was very shy. He never laughed loudly, and he always spoke very softly. And physically he was not as strong as my grandmother. But he excused his lack of physical strength by saying that he was a "**scholar.**"

About three months after their marriage, my grandparents were in a restaurant. A **rascal** began to **insult** my grandfather because he looked weak and had a pretty wife. At first he just made insulting remarks, such as, "Hey! Wet chicken! This is no place for a weakling!"

ASIA
Vietnam

This story takes place in a restaurant in Vietnam, the country where the author was born and grew up.

Key Vocabulary
insult v., to say or do something mean to someone

In Other Words
scholar person who studies a lot
rascal mean person

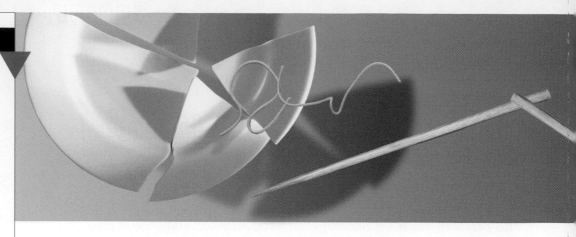

2. Interpret

Underline the phrases that describe how the grandmother reacted in the situation. Would you have reacted the same way? Why or why not?

Possible responses: Yes, I would have reacted the same way. I would not want the rascal to think he could insult me.; No, I would have ignored him. He wasn't worth the trouble of fighting.

3. Irony

Highlight the phrases that show why this scene is ironic. Explain the situation in your own words.

Possible response:

This situation is ironic because the grandmother defended herself and her husband by using karate. I did not expect her to be such a good fighter or to react in this way.

My grandfather wanted to leave the restaurant even though he and my grandmother had not yet finished their meal. But my grandmother pulled his shirtsleeve and signaled him to remain seated. She continued to eat. She looked as if nothing had happened.

Tired of yelling insults without any result, the rascal got up from his table and moved over to my grandparents' table. He grabbed my grandfather's chopsticks. My grandmother immediately **wrested** the chopsticks from him and struck the rascal on his cheekbone with her elbow. The blow was so quick and powerful that he lost his balance and fell on the floor. Instead of finishing him off, as any street fighter would do, my grandmother let the rascal recover from the blow. But as soon as he got up again, he kicked over the table between him and my grandmother. Food and drink flew all over the place. Before he could do anything else, my grandmother kicked him on the chin. The kick was so **swift** that my grandfather didn't even see it. He only heard a heavy thud. Then he saw the rascal tumble backward and collapse on the ground.

> *She looked as if nothing had happened.*

In Other Words
wrested pulled, grabbed
swift quick

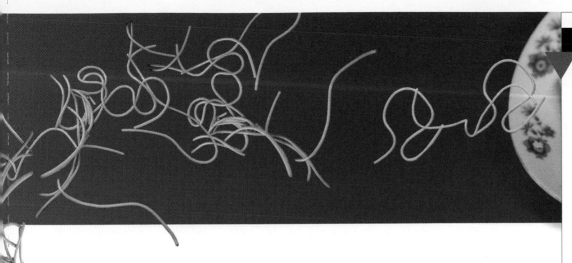

4. Irony
Underline the reaction of the onlookers and then explain why it is ironic.

Possible response: A

person would expect

onlookers and the owner

of the restaurant to be

upset about a fight like

that, but instead they

were happy.

All the <u>onlookers were surprised and delighted</u>, especially the owner of the restaurant. Apparently the rascal, one of the best karate fighters of our area, came to his restaurant every day and left without paying for his food or drink. The owner was too afraid to confront him.

While the rascal's friends tried to **revive him**, everyone else surrounded my grandmother. They asked her who had taught her karate. She said, "Who else? My husband!"

After the fight at the restaurant people **assumed** that my grandfather knew karate very well, but refused to use it for fear of killing someone. In reality, my grandmother had received special training in karate from my great-great uncle from the time she was eight years old.

What is **karate?**

Karate is a form of self-defense that developed long ago in Asia. Traditionally, karate students do not use any weapons. They use their arms and legs to hit and kick opponents.

5. Make Connections
Circle the grandmother's response to the onlookers' question about who taught her karate. Why did she say that? Explain how you were able to figure out the answer.

Possible response: She

said that so her husband

would not be hurt or

embarrassed. I was able

to figure out the answer

by making a connection

to my life. I know I would

do the same thing.

Key Vocabulary
● **assume** *v.*, to think that something is true

In Other Words
revive him wake him up

6. Interpret

What happened as a result of the author's grandmother telling everyone that her husband was one of the best karate fighters? Circle the words and phrases that helped you answer the question.

People started treating

the author's grandfather

with respect.

Anyway, after that incident, my grandfather never had to worry again. Any time he had some business downtown, (people treated him very well.) And whenever anyone happened to bump into him on the street, they bowed to my grandfather in a very respectful way.) ❖

Selection Review Karate

A. Choose one story detail below and explain how using your prior knowledge to make a connection helped you understand the text.

| Detail 1: | All the onlookers were surprised and delighted to see the grandmother kick the rascal. |
| Detail 2: | Everyone assumed the grandfather was an expert in karate, and they treated him with respect. |

Detail: *Possible response:* 1

Prior Knowledge: *Possible response:* I've seen people earn respect for standing up for others. I

know why people treated the grandfather better after that.

B. Answer the questions.

1. How did understanding irony help you appreciate and enjoy this story?

Possible response: The unexpected behavior by the grandmother is an example of irony. I

expected the grandmother to be quiet and afraid, but her actions were totally surprising.

2. Who got what they deserved in this narrative? Explain.

Possible response: The narrator's grandfather received the respect he deserved. The rascal got

what he deserved because he was insulting people for no reason.

Reflect and Assess

WRITING: Write About Literature

A. Plan your writing. How did the characters in each selection respond to insults? List examples in the chart. *Answers will vary.*

Abuela Invents the Zero	Karate
Abuela points her finger at Connie like a judge passing a sentence on a criminal.	

B. How would you advise a good friend to respond to an insult? Write a letter of advice to your friend. Support your views with examples from both texts.

Students should support their letters with examples from the selections.

_____

_____

_____

_____

_____

_____

_____

_____

Integrate the Language Arts

LITERARY ANALYSIS: Analyze Flashback

A **flashback** is a break in the action of a story. It takes the reader back in time to tell about something that already happened. It is used to provide background information about a character or an event. *Answers will vary. Possible responses are shown.*

Example: *It all began with Abuela coming up from the Island for a visit.*

A. Describe the events in "Abuela Invents the Zero" that show a shift in time.

Abuela Invents the Zero
Present: Connie remembers when Abuela said Connie made her feel like a zero.
Flashback: Connie describes Abuela's arrival in the United States, up until the incident that causes Abuela to tell Connie she makes Abuela feel like a zero. Connie gets sent to her room.
Present: The author shifts to the present and says she didn't think about what Abuela said until she was older.

B. List three things that the author's use of flashback in "Abuela Invents the Zero" helped you understand about Connie and her grandmother.

1. Abuela must have been nervous being in such a new place.

2. Abuela raised many children. She is strong in many ways.

3. Abuela has had a difficult life. She suffered and worked hard for her children.

C. Describe how the reader's opinion of Abuela might be different if the author had not used a flashback.

Readers would not be able to sympathize with Abuela. They would never have known how strong Abuela is and how much what Connie did must have hurt her.

VOCABULARY STUDY: Antonyms

Antonyms are words that mean the opposite, or nearly the opposite, of each other. Some antonyms are formed by adding a prefix such as *in-*, *ir-*, or *un-*. For instance, the opposite of *common* is *uncommon*.

A. Read the prefixes in the chart below and write a word you know that contains the prefix.

Prefix	Words I've Used
dis-	dishonest
in-	independent
ir-	irregular
un-	unbelievable

B. Write the words from the chart above and each word's antonym.

Word	Antonym
dishonest	honest
independent	dependent
irregular	regular
unbelievable	believable

C. Use the words you came up with or the word's antonym to write sentences about the characters or events in "Abuela Invents the Zero" or "Karate."

1. The way the grandmother reacts to the rude man at the restaurant was unbelievable.

2. When Abuela first visits the United States, Connie thinks everything about her is irregular.

3. Abuela is honest with Connie about the way she makes her feel.

4. In "Karate," grandmother is very independent and stands up for herself.

Key Vocabulary Review

A. Read each sentence. Circle the word that best fits into each sentence.

1. Someone who is always mean to people is a (**bully**/ **intruder**).

2. If you have a (**positive**/ **sympathetic**) outlook, you see the world in a good way.

3. When you (**insult** /**confront**) someone, you discuss a problem face-to-face.

4. When people send invitations, they often ask for a (**response**/ **reaction**).

5. Waving signs and cheering is one way to help (**challenge** /**motivate**) a team.

6. Someone who is behaving in a goofy or silly manner is being (**ridiculous**/ **defiant**).

7. When you do not pay attention to something, you (**reform** /**ignore**) it.

8. Most plants need water and sunlight for their (**existence**/ **attitude**).

B. Use your own words to write what each Key Vocabulary word means. Then write a synonym for each word. *Answers will vary. Possible responses are shown.*

Key Word	My Definition	Synonym
1. assume	to think something is true	believe
2. attitude	the way you view the world	outlook
3. challenge	to try to get someone to do something	dare
4. defiant	resisting authority	rebellious
5. inconvenient	mildly difficult	troublesome
6. insult	to purposefully be rude or mean to someone	offend
7. intimidate	to act in an aggressive way	threaten
8. sympathetic	showing that you understand the feelings of others	caring

Unit 5 Key Vocabulary

- assume
- attitude
- bully
- challenge

- compromise
- confront
- defiant
- existence

- ignore
- inconvenient
- insult
- intimidate

- intruder
- motivate
- positive
- reaction

- reform
- response
- revelation
- revenge

- ridiculous
- sympathetic
- value
- violence

• Academic Vocabulary

C. Complete the sentences. *Answers will vary. Possible responses are shown.*

1. I show my **reaction** to good news by _smiling and clapping_
   _____ .

2. My school handles student **violence** by _suspending students who get into fights_
   _____ .

3. If I watched a television show about an **intruder**, it would make me feel _nervous about being_
   home alone .

4. One thing I am willing to make a **compromise** about is _what to eat for dinner_
   _____ .

5. The relationship I **value** most in my life is _my relationship with my grandmother_
   _____ .

6. One thing I would choose to **reform** is _the food in the cafeteria_
   _____ .

7. A movie character might seek **revenge** because _someone ruined his life_
   _____ .

8. I was surprised by the **revelation** that _my cousin is a very good cook_
   _____ .

Prepare to Read

▶ 16: The Right Voting Age
▶ Teen Brains Are Different

Key Vocabulary

A. How well do you know these words? Circle a rating for each word. Check your understanding of each word by circling the correct synonym. Then complete the sentences. If you are unsure of a word's meaning, refer to the Vocabulary Glossary, page 764, in your student text.

Rating Scale	
1	I have never seen this word before.
2	I am not sure of the word's meaning.
3	I know this word and can teach the word's meaning to someone else.

Key Word	Check Your Understanding	Deepen Your Understanding
❶ **establish** (i-**sta**-blish) *verb* Rating: 1 2 3	To **establish** something is to _____ it. (**create**) destroy	Things that I can establish include _Possible_ _response:_ bank accounts and e-mail addresses _____ _____ _____ .
❷ **generation** (je-nu-**rā**-shun) *noun* Rating: 1 2 3	A **generation** is an age _____. restriction (**group**)	An experience that I think I will have that my grandparents' generation did not is _Possible response:_ space travel _____ _____ _____ .
❸ **judgment** (**juj**-munt) *noun* Rating: 1 2 3	If you make a **judgment**, you make an _____. effort (**evaluation**)	A person needs to use good judgment when they are _Possible response:_ buying a computer _____ _____ _____ .
❹ **mature** (mu-**choor**) *adjective* Rating: 1 2 3	A **mature** decision is a _____ decision. (**grown-up**) childish	I show that I am mature by _Possible response:_ apologizing for my mistakes _____ _____ _____ .

Key Word	Check Your Understanding	Deepen Your Understanding
5 **participate** (par-**ti**-su-pāt) *verb* **Rating:** 1 2 3	To **participate** in something is to _____ it. (do) avoid	I would like to participate in _Possible response:_ a rock-climbing event _____.
6 **politics** (**pah**-lu-tiks) *noun* **Rating:** 1 2 3	If you talk about **politics**, you are talking about the _____. entertainment (government)	People who are involved in politics include _Possible response:_ the president and senators _____.
7 **qualified** (**kwah**-lu-fīd) *adjective* **Rating:** 1 2 3	A **qualified** person is _____. (experienced) untrained	I can become better qualified for a job by _Possible response:_ doing an internship or taking a class _____.
8 **vote** (vōt) *verb* **Rating:** 1 2 3	To **vote** is to _____. ignore (choose)	I want to vote in order to _Possible response:_ choose a president _____.

B. Use one of the Key Vocabulary words to tell about a responsibility you look forward to having in the future.

Answers will vary.

_____

_____

LITERARY ANALYSIS: Argument and Evidence

In a **persuasive argument**, the writer expresses a strong opinion and uses **evidence**, or proof, to support it. The writer tries to convince readers to agree with his or her opinion.

A. Read the passage below. Write the evidence that supports the writer's opinion in the web.

Look Into the Text

☑ Youths Need the Right to Vote

The National Academies, scientists who write reports for the government, state that 80% of 16- and 17-year-olds work before graduation. The *Houston Chronicle* reports that 61% of teenagers work during the school year. Taxes are taken from these teens' paychecks. But these teens have no say about the ways that tax money is spent.

Details Web

Evidence:
80% of 16- and 17-year-olds work before graduation.

Evidence:
61% of teenagers work during the school year.

Opinion:
Youths need the right to vote.

Evidence:
Teens have no say about the ways their tax money is spent.

Evidence:
Taxes are taken from teens' paychecks.

B. Complete the sentence about the writer's opinion.

The writer's opinion is strong because ___*Possible response:* the writer states his or her opinion___ immediately and then supports it with strong evidence___.

READING STRATEGY: Draw Conclusions

HOW TO DRAW CONCLUSIONS

1. **Identify the Writer's Opinion** Are the opinions based on factual evidence?

2. **Analyze the Evidence** Are the sources reliable?

3. **Decide If the Opinion Is Valid** Does the evidence support the writer's opinion?

A. Read the passage. Use the strategies above to draw conclusions as you read. Then answer the questions below.

Look Into the Text

✔Youths Have Political Knowledge

Young people are learning more about politics than adults. For example, some teens participated in the "We the People" education program. Then they were tested in the areas of government and politics. The results of the testing showed that teens knew as much as or more than adults.

According to the Voting Rights Act of 1965, high school students are qualified to vote. This law states that a sixth-grade education is sufficient for voting. If most 16-year-olds have a tenth-grade education, then they are definitely qualified to vote.

1. What is the writer's opinion about teenage voters?

    The writer thinks that teens should be able to vote when they are 16 because they know just as much as or

    more than adults know about government.

2. Is the writer's opinion valid? Explain why you agree or disagree with the writer's opinion.

    Possible response: Yes. I agree because students learn about voting in school, which helps them become

    more qualified to vote. The Voting Rights Act states that only a sixth-grade education is needed to vote.

    Most teens have a tenth-grade education.

B. Return to the passage above, and circle the words and sentences that helped you answer the first question.

Selection Review 16: The Right Voting Age

EQ **What Rights and Responsibilities Should Teens Have?**
Decide whether teens are mature enough to vote.

A. In "16: The Right Voting Age," you read a persuasive argument that stated why teenagers should have more rights and responsibilities. Complete the diagram with the evidence.

Main-Idea Diagram

> **Writer's Main Argument:**
> The voting age should be lowered to 16.

> **Evidence:**
> Young people who work at age 16 are taxpayers. Sixty-one percent of teenagers work during the school year.

> **Evidence:**
> Young people have the maturity needed to vote. Today, the average age of puberty is about 12.

> **Evidence:**
> Young people have political knowledge. As students, teenagers learn about politics in courses such as history, government, law, and economics.

> **Evidence:**
> Young people want the right to vote. Seventy-three percent of Minneapolis teens support a voting age of 16.

B. Use the information in the diagram to answer the questions.

1. Why did the writer include facts and statistics about young people?

The writer's goal was to persuade readers to agree that the voting age should be lowered. Facts and statistics are evidence, or proof.

2. How might lowering the voting age to 16 affect the next generation's rights and responsibilities? Use **generation** in your answer.

Possible response: Future generations may enjoy more rights and responsibilities once teens are able to vote on issues that are important to them.

3. Do you think 16-year-old teens should be allowed to vote? Explain.

Possible response: Yes. If people can drive cars, hold jobs, and pay taxes, they should be allowed to vote.

Teen Brains Are Different

by Lee Bowman

Connect Across Texts

The National Youth Rights Association uses evidence to support its claim that teens are **mature** and ready for responsibilities. This expository nonfiction presents research to support another view.

Have you ever seen a movie in which a teenager got trapped inside an adult body? Maybe you think the teen can really think and act like an adult. The answer may surprise you.

Teen and Adult Brains

The latest brain research strongly shows that teen brains are very different from adult brains. In teens, parts of the brain related to emotions, **judgment**, and "thinking ahead" are not fully operating. This is one reason why teens show less maturity and control than adults.

Dr. Ruben Gur is a professor of psychology who studies brain behavior. He points out that **impulse control** comes last to the brain and is often the first to leave as people **age**.

How the Brain Matures

Until recently, most brain experts thought that the brain stopped growing by the time a person was about 18 months old. They also thought that the brain **had almost all of its neurons** by age three.

In fact, **the brain's gray matter** has a final period of growth around

According to research, teenagers cannot control their emotions and behavior as well as adults because teens' brains are still growing.

Key Vocabulary
- **mature** *adj.*, like a grown-up
  judgment *n.*, the ability to make good decisions

In Other Words
impulse control being able to think before acting
age get older
had almost all of its neurons was almost developed
the brain's gray matter part of the brain

Interact with the Text

1. Text Structure (Main Idea and Details)
Underline the main idea in column 1. Write one detail that the writer includes to support this main idea.

The parts of the brain

related to emotions,

judgment, and "thinking

ahead" are not fully

operating.

2. Draw Conclusions
Highlight one detail Dr. Ruben Gur gives about impulse control. Think about what you know. Explain what you believe about controlling impulses.

Possible response: I

believe teens are not

always able to control

what they say and do.

3. Interpret

What does this diagram show? Why do you think the author included it?

Possible response: It

shows the parts of the

brain and how the brain

develops. The diagram

is helpful because it

visually explains the

information in the article.

4. Text Structure (Main Idea and Details)

Underline the main idea in column 2. How does it support the main idea of the article?

This supports the

main idea of the article

because it shows why

teen brains are less

developed than adult

brains so teens respond

to things differently than

adults do.

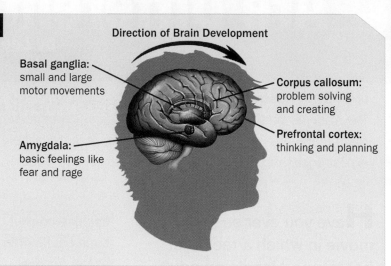

Inside a Teen Brain

The brain grows rapidly before birth and for the first few years of life. A second growth spurt starts around age 12. It lasts through the teen years, when the brain develops gradually from back to front.

Direction of Brain Development

Basal ganglia: small and large motor movements

Corpus callosum: problem solving and creating

Prefrontal cortex: thinking and planning

Amygdala: basic feelings like fear and rage

▲ **Interpret the Diagram** According to this diagram, which part of the brain develops last?

the ages of 11 to 13. This occurs in the front of the brain, an important area for thinking and planning.

These new brain cells do not start working right away, though. It seems to take most of the teen years for them to link to the rest of the brain and to **establish** millions of connections. Only then do the cells allow their owners to think and behave like adults.

At the same time, **adolescent hormones** activate other areas of the brain. The flow of hormones especially affects the amygdala.

This is a simple part of the brain that controls basic feelings like fear and rage.

Different Responses

The result is that teens look at things differently than adults. In a recent study, Deborah Yurgelun-Todd of Harvard Medical School and McClean Hospital noted how teens and adults respond differently to the same pictures. The **subjects** were shown photos of people who looked afraid. The adults named the correct emotion, but the teens seldom did.

Key Vocabulary
● **establish** *v.,* to set up, to create

In Other Words
adolescent hormones natural chemicals in teens' bodies
subjects teens and adults in the study

Yurgelun-Todd and her team repeated the test. This time they **scanned** the subjects' brains. They discovered that the adults and teens used different parts of the brain. Adults used both the advanced front part and the **more primitive** amygdala to process what they had seen. Younger teens used only the amygdala. Older teens **showed a shift toward using** the front part of the brain.

Yurgelun-Todd says that teens may be physically mature. But that does not mean that they can make evaluations as well as adults. "Good judgment is learned," she adds. "But you can't learn it if you don't have the necessary hardware."

Brain Hardware: Use It or Lose It

The development of teen brains involves a process called *myelinization*. During this process, layers of fat cover wire-like nerve fibers that connect parts of the brain. Over time, this helps the brain operate in a more precise and efficient way. It doesn't just affect thinking and problem solving, though. It also impacts body movement and mastery of skills, from throwing a baseball to playing a horn.

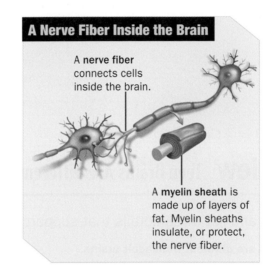

A Nerve Fiber Inside the Brain

A **nerve fiber** connects cells inside the brain.

A **myelin sheath** is made up of layers of fat. Myelin sheaths insulate, or protect, the nerve fiber.

If you don't use your brain cells, they die off. Brain cells that aren't being used don't hook up to other parts of the brain and usually get killed off. "If they're not on the network, they die and their place is taken up with **cerebral fluid**. This goes on well beyond age eighteen," said Dr. David Fassler, a psychiatrist at the University of Vermont.

In Other Words
scanned used special equipment to see
more primitive simpler
showed a shift toward using were different because more of them used
cerebral fluid liquid in and around the brain

5. Text Structure (Main Idea and Details)
Underline the definition and effects of myelinization. Why does the writer include these important details in the article?

The writer includes

these details to explain

the scientific process

of brain development.

Reliable facts support

the main idea.

6. Draw Conclusions
Circle what happens to brain cells if they are not used. Use details from the text and what you know from your own experience to draw a conclusion about why this happens.

Possible response: Brain

cells die if people do not

think or keep their brains

active. Someone who

likes to learn grows new

cells.

7. Interpret

Highlight Dr. Giedd's opinion about teen behavior. Do you agree with his belief that it is important for teenagers to stay active? Why or why not?

Possible response:

Yes. Teens should stay

active so they develop

the thinking abilities

necessary for adulthood.

Dr. Jay Giedd studies brains at the National Institute of Mental Health. He thinks the new understanding of teen brains "argues for doing a lot of things as a teenager. You are **hardwiring** your brain in adolescence," Dr. Giedd says. "Do you want to hardwire it for sports and playing music and doing mathematics, or for lying on the couch in front of the television?" ❖

In Other Words
hardwiring setting up permanent patterns for

Selection Review Teen Brains Are Different

A. Read the main idea, and list three details that support it.

> **Main Idea:** **Teen brains are different from adult brains.**

1. *Possible response:* It takes most of the teen years for new brain cells to establish connections and for teens to think and behave like adults.

2. *Possible response:* Teens could not name the emotion they had when looking at photos, but adults could.

3. *Possible response:* Scans showed teens use different parts of their brains when they respond to things.

B. Answer the questions.

1. Choose one of the details you listed above. Then draw a conclusion about the text based on that detail and what you know.

   Possible response: Some of my friends look old but don't act like adults. Even though teens look mature, they don't always act maturely because their brain cells are still making connections.

2. Based on what you just read, what are two rights and responsibilities younger teens should not have? Why not?

   Possible response: Younger teens shouldn't have the right to vote. They should not have the responsibility of holding a job. Their brains are not developed enough to handle stress.

WRITING: Write About Literature

A. Plan your writing. List reasons from each selection that show why you think teens should or should not be able to vote. *Answers will vary.*

16: The Right Voting Age	Teen Brains Are Different

B. What characteristics do you think make someone a good voter? Review the information you gathered in the chart above, then write a short analysis explaining your answer. Include examples from both texts.

Students should support their answers with examples from the selections.

_____

_____

_____

_____

_____

_____

_____

_____

_____

_____

LITERARY ANALYSIS: Evaluate the Author's Purpose and Perspective

The **purpose** of a persuasive text is to persuade readers to think or take action. Usually, the author has an agenda, or goal. An author of persuasive texts chooses facts that illustrate his or her **perspective**, or point of view.

A. "16: The Right Voting Age" was written by the National Youth Rights Association. Write your ideas about the authors' purpose. Then list the facts given to support the authors' perspective that teens should be able to vote. *Answers will vary.*

Author's Purpose	Supporting Facts

B. Answer the questions. *Answers will vary. Possible responses are shown.*

1. Who is the intended audience for "16: The Right Voting Age"? Why? <u>The article is trying to</u> <u>convince parents and lawmakers that teens are capable of voting. Parents and lawmakers are the people</u> <u>who can make it happen.</u>

2. How did you identify the intended audience? <u>There are many facts and statistics showing why the</u> <u>voting age should be 16. These facts and statistics appeal to audiences who evaluate the laws.</u>

C. Think about another persuasive text you have recently read. Describe the topic. What was the author's purpose and perspective? Who was the intended audience? What agenda do you think the author had?

Answers will vary.

_____

_____

_____

_____

_____

VOCABULARY STUDY: Specialized Vocabulary

Specialized vocabulary words are words that relate to a specific area of study. You can use a dictionary to learn more about the words.

A. The specialized vocabulary words below all relate to brain development. Write what each word means. Check the dictionary for the correct definition, if necessary.

Word	Specialized Definition
adolescent	one who is in the process of growing up
cell	a microscopic mass
hormones	the product of cells circulating through the body, having a stimulating effect
neuron	a specialized cell, a key part of the nervous system

B. The sentences below contain words that relate to the government. Write the specialized definition and the part of speech for each underlined word. Use a dictionary if you need to.

1. American citizens have the <u>right</u> to vote in elections. <u>a power or privilege to which one is entitled;</u> <u>noun</u>

2. When the man lost his case, he made an <u>appeal</u> to the Supreme Court. <u>request to have a case</u> <u>heard again; noun</u>

3. The election of five new members to the <u>House</u> resulted in a majority of Democrats. <u>American legislative body; proper noun</u>

4. The Supreme Court is the highest <u>court</u> in the country. <u>a group with legislative power; noun</u>

C. Write a new sentence using each of the specialized words in Activity B, but use the word with a different meaning. *Answers will vary. Possible responses are shown.*

right _____ I turned right when I should have turned left.

appeal _____ Writers want their books to appeal to readers.

House _____ I want to build a house for my dog.

court _____ Our neighborhood park has one tennis court.

Prepare to Read

▶ Should Communities Set Teen Curfews?
▶ Curfews: A National Debate

Key Vocabulary

A. How well do you know these words? Circle a rating for each word. Check your understanding of each word by circling *yes* or *no*. Then write a definition. If you are unsure of a word's meaning, refer to the Vocabulary Glossary, page 764, in your student text.

Rating Scale	
1	I have never seen this word before.
2	I am not sure of the word's meaning.
3	I know this word and can teach the word's meaning to someone else.

Key Word	Check Your Understanding	Deepen Your Understanding
❶ accountable (u-**kown**-tu-bul) *adjective* **Rating:** 1　2　3	Parents are **accountable** for their young children. (Yes)　　　No	My definition: *Answers will vary.*
❷ authority (u-**thor**-u-tē) *noun* **Rating:** 1　2　3	A student has the **authority** to suspend another student from school. Yes　　　(No)	My definition: *Answers will vary.*
❸ discrimination (dis-kri-mu-**nā**-shun) *noun* **Rating:** 1　2　3	**Discrimination** is about treating everyone fairly. Yes　　　(No)	My definition: *Answers will vary.*
❹ impose (im-**pōz**) *verb* **Rating:** 1　2　3	Teachers **impose** classroom rules that students must follow. (Yes)　　　No	My definition: *Answers will vary.*

Key Word	Check Your Understanding	Deepen Your Understanding
5 **neglect** (ni-**glekt**) *noun* **Rating:** 1　2　3	A clean house shows a homeowner's **neglect**. Yes　　(No)	My definition: *Answers will vary.*
6 **prohibit** (prō-**hi**-but) *verb* **Rating:** 1　2　3	Laws **prohibit** drivers from driving past the speed limit. (Yes)　　No	My definition: *Answers will vary.*
7 **restriction** (ri-**strik**-shun) *noun* **Rating:** 1　2　3	A **restriction** limits a person's activity or freedom. (Yes)　　No	My definition: *Answers will vary.*
8 **violate** (**vī**-u-lāt) *verb* **Rating:** 1　2　3	People are rewarded if they **violate** the law. Yes　　(No)	My definition: *Answers will vary.*

B. Use one of the Key Vocabulary words to write about a right you think teens should have.

Answers will vary.

LITERARY ANALYSIS: Support for an Argument

Writers make a point by stating an opinion and supporting that opinion with evidence. Evidence can include background information, an account of an event, a quote from an expert, and facts.

A. Read the passage below. Complete the chart with evidence that supports the writer's arguments.

Look Into the Text

The Importance of Curfews

Once upon a time, parents weren't afraid to set guidelines or impose restrictions on their children's behavior. They understood that loving their children required setting limits and saying no.

That time is gone. Too many of today's parents just don't want to be responsible for their children.

A case in point: A parent dropped a 12-year-old child off in downtown Orlando at 8 o'clock one morning. At 2 o'clock the following morning, the child was still downtown. That's neglect, plain and simple.

Author's Argument	Evidence
Curfews are important.	In the past, parents set limits and imposed restrictions on their children's behavior.
Parents don't want to be responsible for their children.	A parent left a 12-year-old child downtown alone for 18 hours.

B. Complete the sentence about the writer's argument.

To support her argument, the writer uses evidence such as <u>background information about curfews</u> <u>and a real-life account</u>.

READING STRATEGY: Compare Arguments

HOW TO COMPARE ARGUMENTS

1. **Read** the text.

2. **Identify** the argument.

3. **Look at evidence** to decide if it supports the argument.

A. Read the passage. Use the strategies above to write about the argument and evidence as you read. Then answer the questions below.

Look Into the Text

> So far, I think the curfew is working. The downtown area is safer for kids. Kids aren't being harassed. In fact, the curfew hasn't caused much trouble at all.
>
> The police are doing a very good job. They've been taught how to deal with situations and problems without becoming confrontational. They issue warnings and give kids a certain amount of time to leave. If the kids won't go, police officers pick them up and call their parents.

1. What point is the author trying to make in this passage?

   Curfews are working in her community.

2. What evidence does the author give to support her point?

   The downtown is safer, and kids are not harassed. The police are trained to give kids warnings before they

   pick them up and call their parents.

B. Return to the passage, and reread the evidence. Are you convinced that the evidence supports the argument that curfews are working? Explain.

   Possible response: I think the police are doing a good job, but there are still kids who don't obey the curfew. I

   am not convinced that the curfew is working completely.

Selection Review Should Communities Set Teen Curfews?

EQ **What Rights and Responsibilities Should Teens Have?**
Learn what people think about teen curfews.

A. In "Should Communities Set Teen Curfews?" you read the argument for supporting curfew laws. Complete the web below with evidence from the article.

Details Web

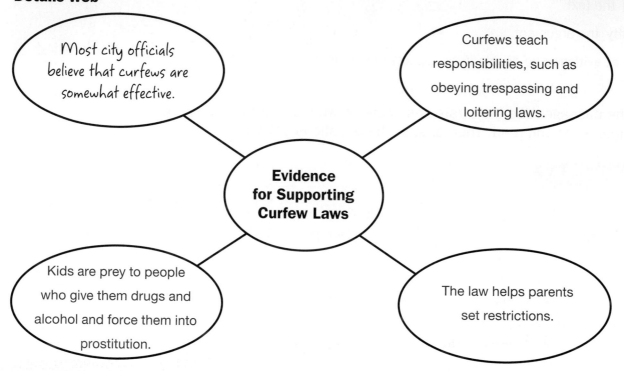

Most city officials believe that curfews are somewhat effective.

Curfews teach responsibilities, such as obeying trespassing and loitering laws.

Evidence for Supporting Curfew Laws

Kids are prey to people who give them drugs and alcohol and force them into prostitution.

The law helps parents set restrictions.

B. Use the information in the web to answer the questions.

1. Why does the writer believe curfew laws are necessary?
Possible response: The writer believes that children are too vulnerable and curfew laws help parents set limits and encourage responsibility.

2. How do curfew laws make parents and teens accountable for a teen's actions? Use **accountable** in your answer.
Possible response: Parents and teens are held accountable for following the curfew laws. If a teen is out after the curfew, the police enforce the laws.

3. Do you think more cities should adopt curfew laws? Why or why not?
Possible response: Cities should adopt curfew laws. The cities that already have curfew laws have seen improvements.

Curfews:
A National Debate

Connect Across Texts

You read arguments in favor of curfews in "Should Communities Set Teen Curfews?" Read the opposite point of view in this persuasive commentary.

In the summer of 1995, the District of Columbia passed a law **imposing** a curfew on teenagers. The law requires everyone under the age of 17 to be home by 11:00 p.m. on weekdays and midnight on weekends. Then they have to stay put until 6:00 a.m. the next morning. The law also **prohibits** drivers under 18 from driving in the District after midnight. Teenagers face punishment if caught in public after curfew. Their parents could be **prosecuted** as well.

In passing this law, Washington, D.C., joined what has become a trend. According to a report in the *American Journal of Police*, 146 of the country's 200 major cities impose curfews of some sort on minors. That's almost 75% of the cities.

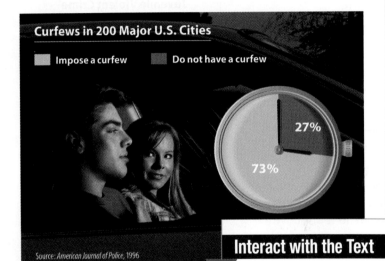

Curfews in 200 Major U.S. Cities

Impose a curfew   Do not have a curfew

27%

73%

Source: American Journal of Police, 1996

Interact with the Text

1. Emotional Appeal
Underline the words and phrases that appeal to your emotions. Explain how these words make you feel about the topic.

Possible response: These words and phrases make me feel that curfew laws are unfair and being forced on people.

Key Vocabulary
- **impose** *v.*, to establish, to apply
- **prohibit** *v.*, to keep people from doing something, to prevent

In Other Words
prosecuted charged by police with breaking the law

2. Compare Arguments
Underline a sentence that supports the writer's position against curfews. Is this evidence reliable and effective? Explain.

Possible response: This statement is not reliable because it is an opinion statement that is not supported by facts or experts.

3. Interpret
Why do you think the writer used the graph in the article? Is it effective?

Possible response: Yes. The writer used the graph because it came from a reliable source and supported the argument well.

Curfews are one of many **misguided** anti-crime strategies. Laws like these **divert** attention from the real causes of crime. The fact is that such laws are **empty political gestures**. They will do nothing to make our streets safer. It is absurd to think that any teenager who is selling drugs or carrying a gun would rush home at 11:00 p.m. to avoid **violating** curfew. Or that this same teenager won't have a false **ID**.

Juvenile Violent Crime

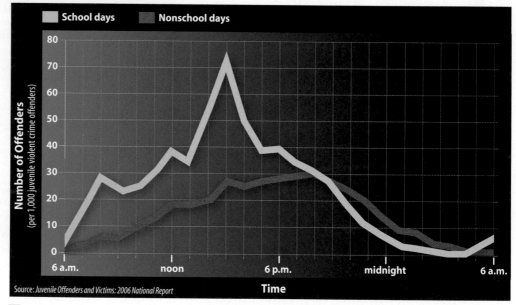

 Interpret the Graph At what time during a school day is juvenile crime most likely to occur?

Certainly any crime that would be committed after midnight can just as easily be committed earlier. In fact, the most active period for juvenile crimes is from noon to 6:00 p.m. on school days.

What curfews will do is **wreak havoc with** the constitutional right to freedom of movement. Curfew laws punish the innocent instead of

Key Vocabulary
● **violate** *v.*, to go against

In Other Words
misguided incorrect, unwise
divert shift
empty political gestures passed so the government looks as if it is being helpful
ID identification card
wreak havoc with ruin, destroy

the guilty. They put law-abiding teenagers under house arrest every night of the week. But it's not because they have done anything wrong. It is because of the crimes committed by others.

Curfews criminalize normal and otherwise lawful behavior. Teenagers can't walk the dog or go for an early morning run during curfew hours. Curfew laws **usurp** the rights of parents to raise their children as they think best. It becomes a crime for parents to allow their teenagers to go to the theater or a jazz club. This law **injects** the government where it doesn't belong.

There is also no evidence that curfews work. In Houston, a curfew was introduced, and youth crime went down by 22%. But in New York, where no curfew exists, youth crime went down 30%. In Detroit and New Orleans, youth crime increased after curfews were introduced. And in San Francisco, youth crime went down after a curfew was **repealed**.

Crime and Curfews

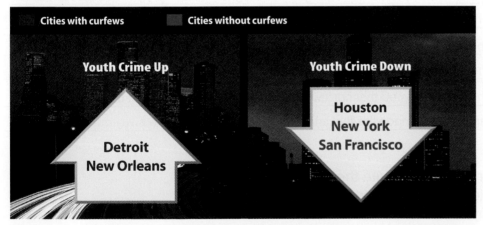

■ **Interpret the Graphic** Which cities have curfews? Does crime always go down when a city has a curfew? How can you tell?

In Other Words
usurp take away
injects puts
repealed removed

Interact with the Text

4. Interpret
Underline the phrases that the writer uses to support the argument that a curfew is like a house arrest. Is this evidence reliable? Why or why not?

Possible response: No.

The writer lists realistic

examples, but they

seem to be exaggerated.

The writer uses loaded

language to appeal to

emotions.

5. Compare Arguments
What argument is the writer trying to make about the relationship between curfews and crime rates? What is your opinion about this argument?

Possible response: The

writer is trying to argue

that there is no solid

relationship between

curfews and low crime

rates. I think there are

other factors that may

explain why crime rates

went up or down.

6. Emotional Appeal

Underline words or phrases about discrimination that appeal to your emotions. Explain why the writer may have included these loaded words.

Possible response:

The writer is trying to

persuade the reader to

agree with the argument

by saying that police

officers discriminate.

Curfews also **squander** police resources that should be used to fight real crime. That is why many police chiefs oppose them.

And inevitably, curfews result in **discrimination**. Studies have consistently found that curfew laws are **disproportionately** enforced in minority communities.

In sum, while curfews may give the appearance of bold action, in reality they do far more harm than good. ❖

Key Vocabulary
• **discrimination** *n.*, treating people unfairly

In Other Words
squander waste
disproportionately unfairly

Selection Review Curfews: A National Debate

A. List three examples of ways the author tried to appeal to your emotions. Use evidence from the text. Explain how these emotional appeals made you feel.

1. *Possible response:* The writer used loaded language like "misguided," "empty political gestures," and "wreak havoc." This language made me feel like the laws might be unnecessary.

2. *Possible response:* The writer used an example of a kid selling drugs and not going home at curfew. This example made me think that curfews can't stop crime or keep teens off the street.

3. *Possible response:* The writer claimed that curfews are the same as house arrest and take away the rights of teens and parents. This made me feel angry that the laws could take away our freedoms.

B. Answer the questions.

1. Compare this writer's argument with the writer's argument from "Should Communities Set Teen Curfews?" Which argument do you agree with? Why?

   Possible response: The writer of the first article used facts and statistics to support the argument. The writer of the second article relied on opinions and loaded language. I agree with the first argument—that kids should have curfews—because that argument was clearly supported.

2. Do you think that curfews interfere with teens' rights, or do they help teens become more responsible? Explain.

   Possible response: I think curfews interfere with teens' rights. Teens should learn responsibility from their parents and their jobs, not from imposed curfews.

Reflect and Assess

WRITING: Write About Literature

A. Plan your writing. Read the opposing opinions. Put an *X* next to the opinion you agree with. Then list examples from each text that support the opinion or oppose it. *Answers will vary.*

☐ **Opinion 1:** Curfews are a good idea.
☐ **Opinion 2:** Curfews are a bad idea.

Should Communities Set Teen Curfews?	Curfews: A National Debate

B. What is your opinion? Write an argument with details from your own experience and evidence from the text.

Students should support their answers with examples from their own experiences and text evidence from the

selections.

_____

_____

_____

_____

_____

_____

Integrate the Language Arts

LITERARY ANALYSIS: Analyze Persuasive Techniques

Persuasive techniques are ways writers persuade readers to believe or to do something. Writers use a variety of persuasive techniques to influence their readers—some can be deceptive, or misleading.

A. Complete the T Chart with ways that each selection tries to persuade readers to believe certain ideas. *Answers will vary. Possible responses are shown.*

T Chart

Should Communities Set Teen Curfews?	Curfews: A National Debate
shows a chart with facts about the curfew times in different cities in order to seem more credible	states many opinions that may or may not be true about the ineffectiveness and political reasons for curfews
uses a picture to help readers imagine a teen walking the streets alone at night	compares the results of curfews in different cities

B. Answer the questions.

1. Which selection do you think was most effective in persuading readers to believe a claim? Why?   "Curfews: A National Debate" was more effective because the statistics about crime rates in different cities seemed credible. The argument against curfews seemed logical to me.

2. Did either of the selections use deceptive techniques to persuade readers? Explain.   I think "Should Communities Set Teen Curfews?" was deceptive because there did not seem to be one credible claim in favor of curfews. It listed the opinions of various city officials to try to persuade readers.

C. Write a brief paragraph to persuade someone to buy what you believe is a great product. Choose a persuasive technique used in one of the selections.

This is a great toothpaste. Since I have been using it, I have gotten many compliments from girls about how nice my teeth look. I can't help but keep smiling. I feel good about myself.

VOCABULARY STUDY: Analogies

An **analogy** is a comparison between two pairs of things. Analogies can show many different relationships, such as objects and their uses, or ideas and their opposites.

A. Read each analogy in the chart below. Then write the type of relationship between the two pairs.

Analogy	Type of Relationship
Blue is to *sky* as *yellow* is to *sun*.	Each pair describes the color of something.
Lion is to *mammal* as *lizard* is to *reptile*.	Each pair shows a specific example of a type of animal.
Laughter is to *happiness* as *tears* are to *sadness*.	Each pair shows what you might do if you were feeling that emotion.
Blocks are to *toys* as *couch* is to *furniture*.	Each pair shows an item in a category.
Black is to *white* as *tall* is to *short*.	Each pair shows an opposite.

B. Complete the analogy.

1. *Dog* is to *bark* as *bird* is to <u>chirp</u>.

2. *Car* is to *road* as *boat* is to <u>water</u>.

3. *Farmer* is to *plow* as *firefighter* is to <u>fire truck</u>.

4. *Legs* are to *walking* as *eyes* are to <u>seeing</u>.

5. *Earrings* are to *ears* as *shoes* are to <u>feet</u>.

C. Create your own analogies below. Each analogy pair is started for you. *Possible responses are shown.*

1. *Clown* is to *joke* as <u>writer is to article</u>.

2. *Winter* is to *summer* as <u>sunshine is to rain</u>.

3. *Short stories* are to *fiction* as <u>biographies are to nonfiction</u>.

4. *Food* is to *hungry* as <u>sleep is to tired</u>.

5. *Golf clubs* are to *golfing* as <u>soccer balls are to soccer</u>.

Prepare to Read

▶ **What Does Responsibility Look Like?**
▶ **Getting a Job**

Key Vocabulary

A. How well do you know these words? Circle a rating for each word. Check your understanding of each word by circling *yes* or *no*. Then complete the sentences. If you are unsure of a word's meaning, refer to the Vocabulary Glossary, page 764, in your student text.

Rating Scale	
1	I have never seen this word before.
2	I am not sure of the word's meaning.
3	I know this word and can teach the word's meaning to someone else.

Key Word	Check Your Understanding	Deepen Your Understanding
❶ afford (u-**ford**) *verb* **Rating:** 1 2 3	Many teens have jobs in order to **afford** things they want to buy. (**Yes**) No	Some things I can afford are ___*Possible response:*___ snacks, CDs, movie tickets _____ _____ _____.
❷ dropout (**drop**-owt) *noun* **Rating:** 1 2 3	A **dropout** is someone who graduates from high school. Yes (**No**)	I do not want to be a dropout because _*Possible*_ _response:_ I want a good job _____ _____ _____ _____.
❸ experience (ik-**spear**-ē-uns) *noun* **Rating:** 1 2 3	**Experience** as a volunteer can help you gain new skills. (**Yes**) No	I learned a lot from an experience I had when _____ *Possible response:* I went on a trip to Africa with my aunt _____ _____.
❹ income (**in**-kum) *noun* **Rating:** 1 2 3	A student might support his family's **income** by working at a store on weekends. (**Yes**) No	One way a teenager can earn an income is by _____ *Possible response:* babysitting _____ _____ _____.

Key Word	Check Your Understanding	Deepen Your Understanding
⑤ independent (in-du-**pen**-dunt) *adjective* **Rating:** 1 2 3	An **independent** person depends on other people to survive. Yes　　(No)	I will be independent when　*Possible response:* I am living on my own and no longer need help from my parents _____ .
⑥ position (pu-**zi**-shun) *noun* **Rating:** 1 2 3	Anyone can be appointed to the **position** of president of a company. Yes　　(No)	In the future, I would like to be appointed to the position of　*Possible response:* school principal _____ .
⑦ reality (rē-**a**-lu-tē) *noun* **Rating:** 1 2 3	**Reality** is how things are at the present moment, not how you want things to be. (Yes)　　No	One reality many teenagers face is　*Possible response:* having too many responsibilities before they are ready _____ .
⑧ reckless (**re**-klus) *adjective* **Rating:** 1 2 3	A **reckless** driver is someone who knows the traffic laws and follows them. Yes　　(No)	I think a reckless person is someone who　*Possible response:* talks on his or her cell phone while driving _____ .

B. Use one of the Key Vocabulary words to write about a responsibility that you currently have.

Answers will vary. _____

_____

LITERARY ANALYSIS: Appeal to Logic

Writers can appeal to your emotions to persuade you to agree with them. Writers also can **appeal to logic**, or reason, as they present an argument.

A. Read the passage below. In the Main-Idea Tree, write the writer's argument and the reasons given to support it.

> **Look Into the Text**
>
> Your plans, you say, are to find a job, get a place of your own, and live your own life. These are understandable goals, but completely unattainable for a 16-year-old dropout.
>
> Buy a copy of today's newspaper and turn to the help-wanted section. Circle the jobs for which you qualify. Notice that high-paying positions require college degrees. Other employers want a high school graduate or GED equivalent. Few bosses will hire those under 18 except as babysitters, ushers, dog-walkers, clerks, or fast-food workers. These jobs pay minimum wage with no benefits and little chance for advancement.

Main-Idea Tree

	A high-paying job requires a college degree.
A 16-year-old dropout cannot earn enough income to live independently.	Other employers want a high school graduate or GED equivalent.
Writer's Argument	Jobs open to those under 18 are minimum wage, with no benefits, and no chance for advancement.
	Reasons

B. Explain how the writer appeals to logic to support her argument.

Possible response: The writer gives facts about the job opportunities available to dropouts. The writer states that if students do not graduate, they will only be able to work at low-paying jobs, and they will not be able to advance.

READING STRATEGY: Form Generalizations

Reading Strategy
Synthesize

HOW TO FORM GENERALIZATIONS

1. **Note details** from the text.

2. **Add examples** about the ideas from your own experience or knowledge.

3. **Make a generalization** that applies to many examples.

4. **Read on** to form more generalizations.

A. Read the passage, and use the strategies above to form generalizations. Then complete the chart.

Look Into the Text

> In addition, landlords demand references. They also want first and last months' rent and a hefty damage deposit before you move in. Many will not rent to minors unless a responsible adult guarantees payment. . . .

Generalization Chart

Details from the Text:
Landlords want references, first and last months' rent, a damage deposit, and a guarantee from an adult if you are a teen.
My Experience:
Possible response: I have older friends who have apartments, and they had to pay a pet deposit if they had a dog or a cat.
Generalization:
Possible response: Renting an apartment when you are a teen is difficult and expensive.

B. Explain how using the strategies helped you to form a generalization.

Possible response: The strategies helped me see how my experience related to the details in the text. Then I could make a generalization about renting an apartment.

Selection Review What Does Responsibility Look Like?

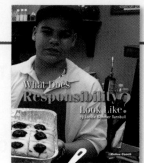

EQ **What Rights and Responsibilities Should Teens Have?**
Read about the reality of adult responsibilities.

A. In "What Does Responsibility Look Like?" you found out what it takes to be independent and responsible. Complete the chart with reasons the writer gives for staying in school. Then summarize the writer's argument.

Reason:	Reason:	Reason:
Only minimum wage jobs are available to high school dropouts.	It is expensive to live alone.	It is dangerous to live in a car or to be homeless.

Writer's Argument:
Many teens want their independence, but it is better to stay in school than to drop out because it is expensive and dangerous for teens to be independent.

B. Use the information in the chart to answer the questions.

1. How does the writer use logic to convince the reader to see her point of view? Is her appeal to logic successful?

   Possible response: The writer presents facts that show how difficult it is for a high school dropout to support himself or herself. She is successful because her logic showed me the reality of dropping out.

2. Do you think teenagers who leave school are reckless? Why or why not? Use **reckless** in your answer.

   Possible response: Yes. It's reckless to throw away the opportunity to get a degree. Getting a degree helps you get a good job.

3. Do you think all dropouts face the same problems that the writer presented? Why or why not? Write a paragraph.

   Answers will vary.

   _____

   _____

   _____

   _____

   _____

   _____

   _____

   _____

   _____

   _____

Getting a Job

Experienced only.

RESTAURANT
F/T Servers needed for downtown restaurant in Lander's Hotel. Dinner shift. Exp req'd. Fax resume and cover to (817) 555-2408 or email landers@towntalk.com

NOW HIRING

187 Meadow Road
Grapevine, TX 76051
March 6, 2007

Dear Sir or Madam:

I was very interested to see your advertisement in yesterday's *Daily Gazette*. I am interested in a career in hotel and restaurant management and would like the opportunity to work in a restaurant like yours.

Although I cannot work full-time right now, I hope that you will still consider me for a job. I have been working for more than a year as a server during the dinner shift. My current **position** has given me a chance to acquire excellent serving skills, and I am eager to develop them more.

I would also value the **experience** of working with your management team and hope that you would consider training me to work with them eventually.

My resume and a letter of recommendation are attached for your consideration.

Sincerely,

Ken Wauneka

Ken Wauneka

Interact with the Text

1. Author's Tone and Purpose
Highlight words and phrases that show the author's tone and purpose. Explain the tone and purpose of this cover letter.

The tone is serious and

respectful, but Ken also

shows eagerness. Ken's

purpose is to apply for

a job.

Key Vocabulary
reality *n.*, the sum of everything real
position *n.*, a specific job
experience *n.*, something you have done, or skills you have learned

Cultural Background
The word *resume* is French. It is often spelled *résumé*, but you may see it without the accents in newspaper ads.

Interactive

2. Form Generalizations

Mark an *X* next to each important detail in this resume. Explain why the author includes these details in his resume.

Possible response: The

author includes these

details to show his

experience and that he

is a hard worker.

KEN WAUNEKA
187 Meadow Road
Grapevine, TX 76051
(817) 555-3965

X **Position Desired:** *Part-Time Server*

X • Dependable • Intelligent • Honest • Hardworking

X **Career Goal:**

Hotel and restaurant management

X **Paid Work Experience:**

Server, Jan. 2006–present
• Work dinner shifts part-time at Green Creek Cafe.

Dishwasher, Busser, Sept. 2005–Dec. 2005
• Worked at El Rancho Restaurant after school and on weekends.

Kitchen Helper, Summers 2003–2005
• Helped clean and **run errands** in my uncle's restaurant, The Desert Diner.

X **Education:**

Will graduate from high school in June 2007.

X **References:**

• *Rita Sando*, Green Creek Cafe manager   (817) 555-4861
• *Lee Wauneka*, owner of The Desert Diner   (817) 555-2699

In Other Words
run errands do small jobs to help

Cultural Background
Every business and area of work has its own jargon, or special vocabulary. Jargon includes words used in a particular way. In the workplace, a *shift* is the full period of time someone works. A *busser* is a worker who sets and clears tables.

GREEN CREEK CAFE

64 Gaylord Street
Grapevine, TX 76051
(817) 555-4861

March 1, 2007

To Whom It May Concern:

I manage the restaurant where Ken Wauneka has been working. He handles a large section of the restaurant during the dinner shift. I am impressed by his skills as a server during this busy, demanding time.

Ken is not only an excellent server, but he has also **mastered** many other duties, such as assisting the cook and **bussing tables**. Ken is a great team player. He always helps his coworkers during **a crunch**.

We will be sorry to lose Ken, but we know that his goal is to become a manager at an establishment like yours. I think Ken would make a great addition to your staff and I highly recommend him.

Sincerely yours,

Rita Sando

Rita Sando
Manager

In Other Words

mastered learned
bussing tables clearing away dirty dishes and setting tables
a crunch the busy times

Interact with the Text

3. Author's Tone and Purpose
Underline words and phrases that show the author's purpose. Explain the purpose of this letter.

The purpose of this letter

is to recommend Ken for

a job.

4. Form Generalizations
Highlight important details in this letter of recommendation. What type of information should this type of document always have?

A recommendation letter

should always show the

author's relationship to

the job applicant, why

the applicant is qualified,

and what kind of

employee he or she is.

5. Form Generalizations

Mark an *X* next to the most important details on this job application. Explain why you think this information is necessary to include on a job application.

Details like this inform

the employer that the

applicant is qualified

and what his intentions

and experience are

for employment. It is

also important for the

employer to know which

position the applicant

wants and how to reach

him.

Lander's
HOTEL AND RESTAURANT
JOB APPLICATION

Date __March 10, 2007__

Tell us about yourself.

X Name __Ken Wauneka__

Street Address __187 Meadow Road__ Apt. _____

City __Grapevine__

State __Texas__ Zip __76051__

Phone __(817) 555-3965__

What position are you applying for? __server__

X What hours and shifts are you interested in?

O Full-time
☑ Part-time

O Breakfast shift
O Lunch shift
☑ Dinner shift

X Have you worked in a restaurant before?

☑ Yes O No

If Yes, turn to page 2 of this application and describe where you worked and what you did. Begin with your most recent position.

— Page 1 —

Position/Duties:

I am a part-time dinner waiter at Green Creek Cafe. I tell customers about the daily specials and take and deliver their orders. At the end of each shift, I help set up the dining room for the next day.

Position/Duties:

I started as a dishwasher at El Rancho Restaurant. When I was promoted to busser, I helped clear and set tables.

Position/Duties:

I was a kitchen helper at The Desert Diner. I cleaned equipment, swept the floors, and ran errands for the cooks.

When can you start work? __March 24, 2007__

— Page 2 —

6. Author's Tone and Purpose
Highlight Ken's duties at the Green Creek Cafe. Why does Ken include these details?

Possible response: He wants the employer to know exactly what he did. The details prove he is qualified.

7. Interpret
Ken sent a resume. Why do you think the employer asks for applicants to fill out an application?

Possible response: The employer wants specific information, which might not be included on a resume. The employer asks for more details to make sure the applicant is qualified.

8. Author's Tone and Purpose

Underline words and phrases that show the author's tone. Explain her tone and purpose.

She is giving information,

but she is also

congratulating her son.

She is excited for him.

Ken,

Ms. Park called from Lander's Restaurant.
She said she enjoyed interviewing you.
She called your references, and
she wants you to start on Saturday!
Congratulations! Call her back
at 555-2408.

—Mom

Selection Review   Getting a Job

A. You read four types of job application documents. Each has a different purpose. Explain the purpose of each document.

1. Cover Letter: It introduces the applicant and explains why he or she wants the job.

2. Resume: It lists the jobs the applicant has had and his or her duties. It also provides his or her level of education.

3. Recommendation Letter: It shows what other employers have thought of the applicant's work and skills.

4. Application: It provides specific information the employer needs.

B. Answer the questions.

1. What should you always do when you apply for a job? List two generalizations.

   Possible response: You should be accurate and give detailed information. You should make sure your tone is appropriate.

2. Imagine that Ken asks you to write a letter of recommendation based on the information he provided on his resume and job application. What information would you include? Why?

   Possible response: I would describe how he shows responsibility as a dinner waiter. I would also include information about Ken's past experiences and how he is qualified for the position.

WRITING: Write About Literature

A. Plan your writing. Think of a job you might want to apply for. What should a cover letter for a job application include? Using "Getting a Job" as a model, list how you want your cover letter to sound and the information you want to include. *Answers will vary.*

Elements of a Cover Letter	My Cover Letter
Tone	
Desired Position	
Experience	
Skills	

B. Using the ideas in the chart above, write a persuasive cover letter to an imaginary employer that explains why they should hire you.

Students should model their cover letters on the cover letter in the selection.

_____

_____

_____

_____

_____

_____

_____

_____

_____

_____

_____

_____

_____

_____

_____

LITERARY ANALYSIS: Evaluate Functional Documents

Functional documents tell how to do something. The information should be clear and easy to follow. If any information is out of order, unclear, or missing, then the document could be useless. *Answers will vary. Possible responses are shown.*

A. In the chart below, explain how each feature of a resume provides important information about the applicant to a potential employer.

Feature	Information
Position Desired	tells the employer exactly which position the applicant wishes to apply for
Goal and Experience	tells the employer if the job applicant has the right skills and experience required for the position
Education	tells the employer if the job applicant has the right level of education required for the position
References	allows the potential employer to talk to others who know the applicant and find out if that person is right for the job

B. Review the features in the chart. Why do you think the information is presented in this order? Is this order logical? Why or why not?

The order makes sense because applicants first describe the position they want, then list their experience

for that position. Then they provide more support by giving references.

C. Write a brief outline of your own resume.

Information students provide should be presented in a logical order.

VOCABULARY STUDY: Multiple-Meaning Words

Many words in English have both an everyday meaning and a special meaning in a career field. These are **multiple-meaning words.**

A. Read each word below. Write its everyday meaning. Use a dictionary to confirm the meaning, if necessary.

Word	Everyday Meaning
benefit	help or useful aid
break	to separate into parts
fire	a burning mass of material
graveyard	cemetery
play	to have fun

B. Read the sentences below. Each sentence contains a word from the chart in Activity A, but the word has a special meaning. Write the special meaning of each underlined word.

Sentence	Special Meaning
Temporary jobs often do not have health and retirement benefits.	a payment or bonus as well as salary
Most people eat lunch on their break.	a short time off work during the day
You might be fired from a job if you arrive late every day.	removed from the job
People who work during the graveyard shift often sleep during the day.	overnight shift
I went to see my friend act in a play.	drama or theatrical work

C. For each word below, write a sentence with an everyday meaning and a specialized meaning. *Answers will vary. Possible responses are shown.*

shift   I need to shift my weight from foot to foot if I stand for too long.

      My dad works the morning shift at the hospital.

pay   My parents pay for my food and clothing.

      The pay at my part-time job allows me to afford the gas I put in my car.

Key Vocabulary Review

A. Use the words to complete the paragraph.

accountable	establish	neglect	restriction
authority	impose	prohibit	violate

Principals and teachers have the _____authority_____ to _____impose_____ rules students must follow.
                (1)   (2)

When students _____violate_____ these rules or _____neglect_____ to follow them, they are held
                (3)   (4)

_____accountable_____ for their actions. Some rules may _____prohibit_____ certain behavior, like wearing
    (5)   (6)

hats in class. Students may feel like these rules are a _____restriction_____ of their rights, but principals
                                          (7)

_____establish_____ most rules to keep students safe.
   (8)

B. Use your own words to write what each Key Vocabulary word means.
Then write a synonym for each word. *Answers will vary. Possible responses are shown.*

Key Word	My Definition	Synonym
1. discrimination	the act of treating people unfairly because they are different	prejudice
2. experience	something you have done or skills you have	skill
3. income	money you earn for working	salary
4. mature	acting grown up	adult or grown-up
5. participate	to take part in	share
6. politics	the activities of the government	government policies
7. position	a certain job or function	role
8. reckless	dangerous or careless	careless

Unit 6 Key Vocabulary

accountable	dropout	• impose	• mature	position	reckless
afford	• establish	• income	neglect	• prohibit	• restriction
• authority	experience	independent	• participate	qualified	• violate
• discrimination	• generation	judgment	politics	reality	vote

• **Academic Vocabulary**

C. Answer the questions using complete sentences. *Answers will vary. Possible responses are shown.*

1. If you could change one aspect of **reality**, what would you change and why?

   I would make it possible for humans to fly because I think it would be amazing to see the world from above.

2. Describe a time when you showed good **judgment**.

   I showed good judgment when I started studying for a math test three days early.

3. Do you think it is important to **vote**? Why or why not?

   Yes, because voting is one way to voice your opinion.

4. Describe a job you are **qualified** to perform.

   I am qualified to work as a waiter because I am friendly and organized.

5. What advice would you give to a high school **dropout**?

   I would tell him or her to go back to school.

6. What makes someone **independent**?

   Someone who is independent can pay his or her bills.

7. What is one thing you wish you could **afford** to do?

   I wish I could afford to visit Africa.

8. How is your **generation** different from your parents' generation?

   We have more freedom and more opportunities.

Prepare to Read

▶ **Novio Boy: Scene 7, Part 1**
▶ **Oranges**

Key Vocabulary

A. How well do you know these words? Circle a rating for each word. Check your understanding of each word by circling *yes* or *no*. Then complete the sentences. If you are unsure of a word's meaning, refer to the Vocabulary Glossary, page 764, in your student text.

Rating Scale	
1	I have never seen this word before.
2	I am not sure of the word's meaning.
3	I know this word and can teach the word's meaning to someone else.

Key Word	Check Your Understanding	Deepen Your Understanding
❶ compliment (**kom**-plu-munt) *noun* **Rating:** 1 2 3	A person can give a **compliment** as a way to show appreciation and admiration. (**Yes**) No	One compliment I have received lately is _Possible_ _response:_ that my hair looks nice _____ _____ _____ .
❷ conceal (kun-**sēl**) *verb* **Rating:** 1 2 3	The best way to **conceal** a secret is to tell everyone you know. Yes (**No**)	Famous people sometimes conceal their appearance by _Possible response:_ wearing big sunglasses and baseball caps _____ _____ .
❸ elegance (**e**-li-guns) *noun* **Rating:** 1 2 3	Dancers move with grace, beauty, and **elegance**. (**Yes**) No	When I think of elegance, I think of _Possible responses:_ a fancy hotel, a queen, an expensive evening gown _____ _____ .
❹ nervous (**nur**-vus) *adjective* **Rating:** 1 2 3	A **nervous** person feels confident, assured, and eager. Yes (**No**)	One thing that makes me feel nervous is _Possible_ _response:_ shooting a free throw during a tied basketball game _____ _____ .

Key Word	Check Your Understanding	Deepen Your Understanding
5 overprotective (ō-vur-pru-**tek**-tiv) *adjective* **Rating:** 1 2 3	Taking someone with a paper cut to the emergency room is an example of **overprotective** behavior. (**Yes**) No	Children of overprotective parents may react by _____ *Possible response:* rebelling against their parents' rules _____ _____ _____ .
6 personality (pur-su-**na**-lu-tē) *noun* **Rating:** 1 2 3	Spending time with someone is a good way to find out what kind of **personality** they have. (**Yes**) No	I would describe my personality as *Possible response:* outgoing and friendly _____ _____ _____ _____ .
7 reveal (ri-**vēl**) *verb* **Rating:** 1 2 3	When you **reveal** the truth, you keep it secret. Yes (**No**)	When I first meet someone, I don't like to reveal _____ *Possible response:* personal details about myself _____ _____ _____ .
8 romantic (rō-**man**-tik) *adjective* **Rating:** 1 2 3	**Romantic** movies are suspenseful and violent. Yes (**No**)	Romantic songs make me feel *Possible response:* _____ happy and dreamy _____ _____ _____ _____ .

B. Use one of the Key Vocabulary words to write about a situation where you made a good impression on someone.

Answers will vary. _____

_____

Before Reading Novio Boy: Scene 7, Part 1

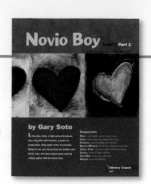

LITERARY ANALYSIS: Dramatic Elements

A **play** is a story performed by actors. Plays have **dramatic elements**, such as **scenes** or **acts**, **dialogue**, and **stage directions**. These elements help you understand the characters, the setting, and the action.

A. Read the passage below. Complete the chart with examples of each character's dialogue and actions.

> ### Look Into the Text
>
> **WAITER.** [*looking up happily*] Mademoiselle and monsieur. Please take this seat by the window. [*pulls chair out for* PATRICIA]
>
> **PATRICIA.** [*sniffs the flower on the table*] It's so romantic. So sophisticated, so charming, so . . . And look, a guitarist!
>
> [RUDY *sees that it's his* UNCLE JUAN, *who waves at him.* RUDY *shakes his head at his* UNCLE, *as if to say, Don't say anything.*]
>
> **PATRICIA.** It's a discriminating restaurant.
>
> **RUDY**: Do they discriminate against Latinos? If so, I ain't going to eat here. We'll go grub at Pollo Loco instead.
>
> **PATRICIA.** No, Rudy. It's just a very fine restaurant. And look, cloth napkins. How fancy!
>
> **RUDY.** [*studies napkins*] Looks like a diaper.
>
> **PATRICIA.** Rudy, you're so silly.

Dramatic Element	Example 1	Example 2
Dialogue	"It's so romantic. So sophisticated, so charming, so . . . And look, a guitarist!"	"Do they discriminate against Latinos? If so, I ain't going to eat here."
Stage directions	sniffs the flower on the table	Rudy shakes his head at his uncle, as if to say, Don't say anything.

B. What do you learn about the characters from their dialogue and the stage directions?

Possible response: Patricia is romantic and is very excited to be at such a fancy restaurant. Rudy is worried they might be discriminated against, and he is embarrassed that his uncle is working at the restaurant.

READING STRATEGY: Form Mental Images

HOW TO FORM MENTAL IMAGES

1. **Find Clues** Look for words that describe the characters and events.

2. **Visualize** Use the descriptive words to create pictures in your mind.

3. **Sketch** Draw pictures to show what is happening.

A. Read the passage. Use the strategies above to form mental images as you read. Answer the questions below.

Look Into the Text

[JUAN *starts playing his guitar and singing.* RUDY *and* PATRICIA *listen.*
   Silly song, perhaps "Tort y Frijoles."]

PATRICIA. He's really talented.

RUDY. He's OK.

WAITER. [*approaches with glasses of water*] Our special for the day is . . .
   [*A "mooooo" sounds.*]

WAITER. [*continuing*] . . . tender veal. We have spotted cow, brown cow,
   black-and-white cow, and—
   [*The mooing sounds again.*]

WAITER. I'll be back to get your order. I have to see about something
   in the kitchen. [*leaves, pulling a meat cleaver from belt*]

PATRICIA. The food's really . . .

PATRICIA. . . . fresh.

1. **Which words and phrases describe the characters and events?**

   Juan starts playing his guitar and singing. Rudy and Patricia listen. Silly song. The waiter approaches with

   glasses of water. A "mooooing" sound starts. The waiter leaves, pulling a meat cleaver from belt.

2. **How do you visualize the scene in your mind?**

   Possible response: I see Juan playing the guitar and Patricia watching him and maybe humming along. I see

   the waiter bring glasses and getting frustrated by the sounds coming from the kitchen. Rudy and Patricia

   probably have confused looks on their faces, especially when the waiter pulls a meat cleaver out of his belt.

B. How did finding descriptive words and phrases help bring the scene to life?

   Possible response: Finding the action words helped me see what the characters were doing. The descriptive

   phrases helped me hear what was going on and understand Patricia and Rudy's confusion at the sounds.

Selection Review Novio Boy: Scene 7, Part 1

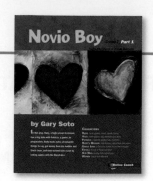

EQ ## What Do You Do to Make an Impression?
Read about teens who are nervous on a first date.

A. In "Novio Boy: Scene 7, Part 1," Rudy and Patricia try to impress each other on their first date. In the Cause-and-Effect chart, write what the characters do and say and what effect their actions have.

Cause-and-Effect Chart

What the Characters Do and Say	What Impression They Make
Rudy takes Patricia to a nice restaurant.	Patricia is excited to be there and that Rudy would pick such a nice place.
Patricia compliments the restaurant and then tells Rudy he is silly.	Rudy feels comfortable and less nervous.
Rudy asks about her pin and her cat.	Patricia is flattered that Rudy would notice her pin and ask about it.
Patricia orders a huge meal.	Rudy is worried he doesn't have enough money. He orders crackers.
Patricia compliments Rudy and says he is daring, intelligent, and loyal.	Rudy is embarrassed but happy she said those things.
Rudy reads a list of compliments he wrote about her.	Patricia thinks Rudy is sweet and is happy that he compliments her, but she knows it didn't come from the heart.
Patricia offers to share her meal with Rudy.	Rudy thinks she's nice and generous.

B. Use the information in the chart on page 242 to answer the questions.

1. Based on their actions and words, what impression do you think Patricia and Rudy have of each other? Explain.

   Possible response: I think Patricia thinks Rudy is sweet, but shy. I think she likes him because she keeps

   saying nice things to him. Rudy really likes Patricia and thinks she is pretty and nice. He seems worried

   that she won't like him, so he keeps trying to do things that will make Patricia like him.

2. How would you describe Patricia's personality? Use **personality** in your answer.

   Possible response: Patricia has a kind and generous personality. She compliments Rudy and is happy to

   share her fries with Rudy. She is energetic, friendly, and outgoing.

3. Reread the part of the play where Rudy compliments Patricia. How do you visualize this scene? Make a sketch of the scene. Then describe it in your own words below.

Answers will vary.

Interactive

Connect Across Texts

In Part 1 of Novio Boy, *you read about the beginning of Rudy and Patricia's date. Read about another first date in this narrative poem.*

Oranges
by Gary Soto

The first time I walked
With a girl, I was twelve,
<u>Cold</u>, and weighted down
With two oranges in my jacket.
5   <u>December. Frost cracking</u>
Beneath my steps, my breath
Before me, then gone,
As I walked toward
<u>Her house, the one whose</u>
10 <u>Porch light burned yellow</u>
Night and day, in any weather.
A dog barked at me, until
She came out pulling
At her gloves, face bright
15 With rouge. I smiled,
Touched her shoulder, and led
Her down the street, across
A <u>used car lot</u> and a line
Of newly planted trees,

Classic Tiles Composition II, 2001, Ger Stallenberg.
Oil on canvas, private collection, the Netherlands.

▲ **Critical Viewing: Effect** How does the mood in this painting relate to the poem? How is it different from the poem?

In Other Words
rouge blush, red makeup

20　Until we were breathing
　　Before a drugstore. We
　　Entered, the (tiny bell)
　　Bringing a saleslady
　　Down a (narrow aisle of goods.)
25　I turned to the (candies)
　　(Tiered like bleachers,)
　　And asked what she wanted—
　　Light in her eyes, a smile
　　Starting at the corners
30　Of her mouth. I fingered
　　A nickel in my pocket,
　　And when she lifted a chocolate
　　That cost a dime,
　　I didn't say anything.
35　I took the nickel from
　　My pocket, then an orange,
　　And set them quietly on
　　The counter. When I looked up,
　　The lady's eyes met mine,
40　And held them, knowing
　　Very well what it was all
　　About.

　　　　Outside,
　　A few cars hissing past,

In Other Words
Tiered Placed, Arranged
fingered felt

Interact with the Text

1. Narrative Poetry
Underline words and phrases on page 244 that describe the setting. Describe the setting in your own words.

Possible response: It is a cold day in December, with frost on the ground.

2. Form Mental Images
Circle details about the drugstore. Describe how you visualize the store.

Possible response: I see the drugstore as a small, crowded shop with colorful piles of candy.

3. Narrative Poetry
Highlight how the boy pays for the candy and how the saleslady reacts. What does this tell you about the characters?

Possible response: The boy does not have much money. She understands and accepts his payment. She is kind and will not embarrass him.

Integrate the Language Arts

LITERARY ANALYSIS: Compare Literature

Drama and poetry are two different **genres**, or types of literature. An author's choice of genre affects how the **theme**, or message, is expressed.

A. In a play, theme is frequently revealed through dialogue and action. Read the examples below and write the message that the lines reveal.

Dialogue	What It Reveals
RUDY. [*notices her jewelry*] That's a cute cat pin.	Rudy says what's on his mind.
PATRICIA. I mean, you're nicer than most boys, and not stupid, either.	Patricia likes Rudy because he's different from other boys.
PATRICIA. Sounds weird, but I like my fries with mustard. **RUDY.** Yeah? Me, too.	You can discover how much you have in common with someone when you are honest.
ALEX. Forget the notes. Speak from your heart.	You don't need a script to talk to someone you like. You should just tell them how you feel.

What is the theme? It's always best to be yourself.

B. Poets often choose words because of the images they create or because they have a particular sound. Answer the questions about "Oranges." *Answers will vary.*

1. List two strong images from the poem.

_____

_____

2. What messages do these images communicate?

_____

_____

3. What is the theme of the poem?

_____

_____

C. Can you learn more about the theme from dialogue and action, or from description and word choice?

Answers will vary.

_____

_____

VOCABULARY STUDY: Idioms

An **idiom** is a group of words that have a different meaning than the literal meaning. Context clues can help you figure out the meaning of an idiom.

A. Read the underlined idioms below. Use context clues to help you figure out the meaning of each idiom. Then write what you think the idiom means.

Idiom	What I Think It Means
Rudy hopes Patricia's parents do not come into the restaurant. If they do, he will be <u>out of the frying pan and into the fire</u>.	Rudy will be in even more trouble.
Rudy doesn't order much food because everything on the menu <u>costs an arm and a leg</u>.	Everything is very expensive.
Patricia thinks the cloth napkin is elegant, but Rudy <u>could take it or leave it</u>.	Rudy does not care about the napkin.
Rudy wants to compliment Patricia, but he <u>goes overboard</u> when he reads lines from a notebook.	His actions are too extreme.

B. Complete the following sentences with context clues. The underlined phrases are idioms.

1. I'm <u>hungry enough to eat a horse</u> because <u>I haven't had anything to eat since breakfast.</u>

2. She hoped no one was planning to <u>spill the beans</u> about <u>the surprise party.</u>

3. He was <u>up the creek with no paddle</u> when his computer <u>broke down right before his paper was due.</u>

4. It was time to <u>get the show on the road</u> because <u>we were really late and needed to be on time.</u>

C. Write a short paragraph containing two idioms you know that do not appear above.

Paragraphs should reflect understanding of the idioms.

Unit 7
Pages 550–567

Prepare to Read
▶ Novio Boy: Scene 7, Part 2
▶ Your World

Key Vocabulary

A. How well do you know these words? Circle a rating for each word. Check your understanding of each word by circling the correct synonym. Then complete the sentences. If you are unsure of a word's meaning, refer to the Vocabulary Glossary, page 764, in your student text.

Rating Scale	
1	I have never seen this word before.
2	I am not sure of the word's meaning.
3	I know this word and can teach the word's meaning to someone else.

Key Word	Check Your Understanding	Deepen Your Understanding
❶ ashamed (u-**shāmd**) *adjective* **Rating:** **1 2 3**	If you feel **ashamed**, you feel _____. (**guilty**) proud	I would feel ashamed if I *Possible response:* cheated on a test _____ _____ _____ .
❷ conscious (**kon**-shus) *adjective* **Rating:** **1 2 3**	If you make a **conscious** decision, you make a _____ decision. casual (**deliberate**)	An example of a time I made a conscious decision is when I *Possible response:* ran for class president _____ _____ _____ .
❸ desire (di-**zīr**) *noun* **Rating:** **1 2 3**	A **desire** is a _____. need (**wish**)	One desire I have for next year is *Possible response:* to get a part in the school play _____ _____ _____ .
❹ flirt (**flurt**) *verb* **Rating:** **1 2 3**	To **flirt** is to act in a way that shows you _____ someone. (**like**) fear	In movies, people flirt with each other by *Possible* *response:* smiling and complimenting each other _____ _____ _____ .

250 **Unit 7:** Making Impressions

Key Word	Check Your Understanding	Deepen Your Understanding
5 horizon (hu-**rī**-zun) *noun* **Rating:** 1 2 3	If you see the **horizon**, you see the _____. (**skyline**)　　**stars**	The best place to see the horizon is _Possible_ *response:* on the beach or a hilltop _____ _____ _____ .
6 privacy (**prī**-vu-sē) *noun* **Rating:** 1 2 3	Someone who values their **privacy** values their _____. (**solitude**)　　**openness**	You can respect someone's privacy by _Possible_ *response:* knocking before you enter their room _____ _____ _____ .
7 recover (ri-**ku**-vur) *verb* **Rating:** 1 2 3	To **recover** something is to _____ it. **adapt**　　(**regain**)	If I wanted to recover as quickly as possible from a cold, I would _Possible response:_ rest, sleep, and take vitamins _____ _____ .
8 reluctant (ri-**luk**-tunt) *adjective* **Rating:** 1 2 3	If you feel **reluctant**, you feel _____. **confident**　　(**uncertain**)	Something I am reluctant to try is _Possible response:_ bungee jumping _____ _____ _____ .

B. Use one of the Key Vocabulary words to write about what you do that gives you confidence.

Answers will vary.

_____

_____

Before Reading Novio Boy: Scene 7, Part 2

LITERARY ANALYSIS: Characters and Plot in Drama

In a play, the playwright uses **dialogue**, the **set**, and **stage directions** to reveal details about the **characters** and **plot**.

A. Read the passage below. Look for stage directions and dialogue that tell you about each character. Then complete the chart.

Look Into the Text

> [RUDY, *straightening the collar of his shirt, returns to the table*;
>   PATRICIA *hurries to the table as well.*]
> **PATRICIA.** Is he a friend of yours?
> **RUDY.** Kind of. [*pause*] Patricia, you got a . . . complex personality.
>   I mean, you're not stuck-up. You're willing to go out with a boy
>   who . . .
> **PATRICIA.** What?
> **RUDY.** [*shyly*] Never mind.
> **PATRICIA.** Come on, tell me.
> **RUDY.** Who still has his G.I. Joes.
> **PATRICIA.** You're cute! [*pause*] You know, I saw you play baseball
>   before.

Character	What the Character Says and Does
Rudy	straightens his collar tells Patricia she has a complex personality speaks shyly
Patricia	hurries to the table tells Rudy he's cute, and she's seen him playing baseball

B. Complete the sentence about Rudy and Patricia.

Rudy and Patricia are both nervous about being on a date together. He doesn't understand why she went out with him, but she thinks he is cute.

READING STRATEGY: Identify Sensory Images

HOW TO IDENTIFY SENSORY IMAGES

1. **Look for sensory images** or words that tell you how things look, sound, smell, taste, and feel.

2. **Imagine the scene** and what you see, hear, smell, taste, and touch.

A. Read the passage. Use the strategies above to identify sensory images as you read. Then answer the questions below.

Look Into the Text

> **ALEX**. *Mira*, she left a French fry. Here, Novio Boy. [*feeds it to RUDY*]
>
> **RUDY**. She wiped me out for the rest of ninth grade. But it beats doing nothing.
>
> [*At this*, JUAN *begins to play a song about "nothing."*]
>
> **RUDY**. Thanks for helping out, unc.
>
> **JUAN**. *No problema.* You're my only nephew. About the money . . . You can pay me back later.
>
> **ALEX**. But me first.
>
> [JUAN *returns to his stool and starts strumming his guitar softly.*]

1. What do you see, hear, smell, taste, and touch? Complete the chart with your responses to the text.

My Response to the Text	
I see: Alex, Juan, and Rudy talking. Alex feeds Rudy a fry. Juan plays the guitar.	**I smell:** French fries and other food
	I taste: French fries
I hear: Juan playing a song on his guitar.	**I feel:** Alex feeding a fry to Rudy

2. How do these sensory images help you experience the story?

   Possible response: The sensory images help me feel like I am in the scene with the characters and experiencing what they are experiencing.

B. Return to the passage above, and circle the words or sentences that helped you answer the first question.

Selection Review Novio Boy: Scene 7, Part 2

EQ **What Do You Do to Make an Impression?**
Read about people who gain confidence in themselves.

A. In Part 2 of "Novio Boy," Rudy's friends and family help him gain
confidence in himself. Complete the chart with examples of dialogue
and stage directions that give you new information about each of the
characters.

Rudy	Patricia
pulls his notepad from his pocket and reads from it	"No, but I liked how you tried really hard."
He is shocked but quickly recovers.	"Let's dance, Rudy."
"Dance? No, I'm too full."	She tries to dance close to him.
"How come you're spying on me?"	"We can split this . . . Oh, wait! I'll pay the tip!"
"I'm gonna have a yard sale, so I can earn back what I owe you and Mom and Uncle."	Gives Rudy a kiss on his cheek.

Rudy's Mom	Alex
Rudy's mother shushes Estela, and they hide behind menus so Rudy won't see them.	"I'll help you out. I got some stuff underneath my bed."
"Cross my heart. I didn't know, really."	"We ninth graders got to stick together."
"What, are you embarrassed? Ashamed of your mommy?"	They shake hands elaborately.
"She's a good girl. But I don't want you driving a car with her."	"Man, it's tough being a Novio Boy."

B. Use the information in the chart to answer the questions.

1. Think about the characters' actions and dialogue. What new
information do you learn about Rudy?

Rudy is nervous and afraid to dance in front of his mom. He is also honest because he is willing to sell his

things to pay back the people who help him. The other characters care about him.

2. Rudy's mom asks if he is ashamed of her. Why do you think she asks
him that? Use **ashamed** in your response.

Possible response: Rudy's mom wants Rudy to realize that he should not be ashamed. She can tell that

Patricia likes him and isn't judging him.

3. How do you think Rudy would act if he goes out with Patricia again?

Possible response: Rudy won't be as nervous or embarrassed because he has more confidence. He will

probably be more natural and not read from notes.

Connect Across Texts

In Part 2 of Novio Boy, *Rudy becomes more confident. Read this poem about another person who is* **reluctant** *at first but then changes.*

Your World

by Georgia Douglas Johnson

Your world is as big as you make it.
I know, for I used to abide
In the narrowest nest in a corner,
My wings pressing close to my side.

5 But I sighted the distant horizon
Where the skyline encircled the sea
And I throbbed with a burning desire
To travel this immensity.

   I battered the cordons around me
10 And cradled my wings on the breeze
   Then soared to the uttermost reaches
   With rapture, with power, with ease!

Key Vocabulary
- **reluctant** *adj.*, unsure, unwilling
  horizon *n.*, the line where the sky
    and land or water seem to meet
  desire *n.*, something that you
    want strongly; a wish

In Other Words
abide live
encircled went all around
immensity huge place
battered the cordons broke the ties
rapture happiness

Interact with the Text

1. Use Sensory Images to Understand
Underline the descriptive phrases that helped you experience what the poet is describing. How do they affect your understanding of the poem?

Possible response: These

words helped me visualize

a bird breaking free of

his nest and soaring

through the sky. It helped

me understand how

the speaker feels about

freedom and everyone's

right to have it.

Selection Review Your World

A. Complete the chart with sensory images from the poem and your experiences.

What I Read	What I Experience
"My wings pressing close to my side."	I feel like I'm trapped in a small space.
"Where the skyline encircled the sea"	I see a beautiful horizon. The sky seems to touch the water.
"I throbbed with a burning desire"	I feel my heart beating and wanting to escape and be free.
"cradled my wings on the breeze"	I feel peaceful like I am floating.
"Soared to the uttermost reaches"	I see the world far below me and feel strong, powerful, and free.

B. Answer the questions.

1. How did rhyme and rhythm help you understand the poem?

Possible response: The rhyme and rhythm made the poem easier to read because there was a pattern. The rhythm of the poem made the images clearer and more meaningful.

2. Describe what it would be like to meet the speaker in this poem. Use details from the poem to support your answer.

Possible response: I think I would have things in common with her because she seems hesitant to take risks, but once she makes a decision she does not look back.

Reflect and Assess

WRITING: Write About Literature

A. Plan your writing. Read the first line of "Your World" below. Decide whether you agree or disagree with it. List evidence from both texts that supports your choice. *Answers will vary.*

Your world is as big as you make it.

Novio Boy: Scene 7, Part 2	Your World

B. Write an explanation and comment about the first line of "Your World." Support your comment using your own opinion and evidence from both texts.

Students should support their answers with examples from the selections and their own opinions.

_____

_____

_____

_____

_____

_____

_____

_____

_____

LITERARY ANALYSIS: Rhythm and Meter

Rhythm is the pattern of beats that gives poetry its musical quality. The repetition of sounds is one form of rhythm. Another form is **meter**. Meter is a pattern of stressed and unstressed syllables in a line of poetry. A **foot** is a unit of stressed and unstressed syllables.

A. Read the lines below from "Your World" and mark each stressed syllable with a ´ and mark each unstressed syllable with a ˘.

> I battered the cordons around me
> And cradled my wings on the breeze
> Then soared to the uttermost reaches
> With rapture, with power, with ease!

B. In the lines below, mark each unstressed syllable with a ˘. Then mark each stressed syllable with a ´.

> Your world is as big as you make it.
> But I sighted the distant horizon.

What do you notice about the pattern of these two lines above?

Possible response: The pattern is relatively the same.

C. Write a short poem with a specific rhythm and meter. You can use the same meter as "Your World," or make up a different pattern of stressed and unstressed syllables.

Answers will vary.

VOCABULARY STUDY: Idioms

Idioms mean something different from the literal, or exact, meanings of their words. To figure out the meaning of an unfamiliar idiom, you can study the context of the phrase, or predict the meaning, and then test your prediction.

A. Read the idioms that are underlined in the chart below. Write what you think each idiom means, then identify the strategy that you used to figure out the meaning.

Idiom	What I Think It Means	Strategy
Amanda was a <u>back-seat driver</u>, shouting out instructions along the way.	She was giving orders to the driver.	context
I had to stop dancing because I got a <u>Charley horse</u> in my left leg.	a cramp	context
It didn't matter which choice she made, they were both a <u>catch-22</u>.	no-win situation	prediction
Lily's baby girl was as <u>cute as a kitten</u>.	adorable	context

B. Read the excerpt from "Novio Boy." Write how you used each step to figure out the meaning of the underlined idiom. *Answers will vary. Possible responses are shown.*

> **RUDY.** How come you're spying on me?
> **MOTHER.** I'm not, m'ijo! Me and Estela came here to hear your uncle . . .
> **RUDY.** You're snooping! I know you are!
> **MOTHER.** <u>Cross my heart.</u> I didn't know, really.

1. Study the context of the phrase.

The text before the idiom shows that Rudy's mother is denying his accusation.

2. Predict the meaning.

I think she is promising that she is not spying.

3. Test your prediction.

The text immediately after the idiom supports my prediction.

C. Complete the sentence containing the idiom "I wash my hands of it."

If my brother can't keep his room clean, I wash my hands of it because   *Possible response:* I am

not the one who should be responsible for his messy bedroom.

Prepare to Read

▶ **To Helen Keller**
▶ **Marked/Dusting**

Key Vocabulary

A. How well do you know these words? Circle a rating for each word. Check your understanding of each word by circling *yes* or *no*. Then write a definition. If you are unsure of a word's meaning, refer to the Vocabulary Glossary, page 764, in your student text.

Rating Scale

1 I have never seen this word before.

2 I am not sure of the word's meaning.

3 I know this word and can teach the word's meaning to someone else.

Key Word	Check Your Understanding	Deepen Your Understanding
❶ anonymous (u-**no**-nu-mus) *adjective* **Rating:** 1 2 3	An **anonymous** letter is unsigned. (**Yes**) No	My definition: *Answers will vary.*
❷ conquer (**kon**-kur) *verb* **Rating:** 1 2 3	You can sometimes **conquer** a fear by doing what you are afraid of. (**Yes**) No	My definition: *Answers will vary.*
❸ contribute (kun-**tri**-byūt) *verb* **Rating:** 1 2 3	A volunteer does not **contribute** time or effort. Yes (**No**)	My definition: *Answers will vary.*
❹ encouragement (in-**kur**-ij-munt) *noun* **Rating:** 1 2 3	Fans give their team **encouragement** by booing. Yes (**No**)	My definition: *Answers will vary.*

Key Word	Check Your Understanding	Deepen Your Understanding
⑤ imperfection (im-pur-**fek**-shun) *noun* **Rating:** 1 2 3	A used car never has an **imperfection**. Yes (No)	My definition: _*Answers will vary.*_ _____ _____ _____ _____
⑥ inspire (in-**spīr**) *verb* **Rating:** 1 2 3	Before a game or competition a coach tries to **inspire** the players. (Yes) No	My definition: _*Answers will vary.*_ _____ _____ _____ _____
⑦ overcome (ō-vur-**kum**) *verb* **Rating:** 1 2 3	You can **overcome** a problem by working hard to solve it. (Yes) No	My definition: _*Answers will vary.*_ _____ _____ _____ _____
⑧ unforgettable (un-fur-**ge**-tu-bul) *adjective* **Rating:** 1 2 3	An **unforgettable** experience is something you do not remember. Yes (No)	My definition: _*Answers will vary.*_ _____ _____ _____ _____

B. Use one of the Key Vocabulary words to describe how you want to be remembered.

Answers will vary.
_____
_____

Before Reading To Helen Keller

LITERARY ANALYSIS: Style

A writer's **style** is the particular way he or she writes. Word choice and sentence structure help create a writer's style.

A. Read the passage below. Complete the chart with the effects that the writer's word choice and sentence structure have.

> **Look Into the Text**
>
> She,
> In the dark,
> Found light
> Brighter than many ever see.

Word Choice	Sentence Type
Possible response: The simple, everyday words make the ideas easy to understand. The subject of the poem seems like she will be an ordinary person.	*Possible response:* The complex sentence structure makes the text seem very visual and dramatic. It hints at how complex her life might be.

B. Complete the sentence about the writer's style. Use an example of the poet's words to explain your answer.

The writer's style is   *Possible response:* both straightforward and dramatic. He says a lot with a few words.
The line breaks make readers pause and think about the meaning. Phrases such as "In the dark" and "Found light" are very simple but very dramatic.

READING STRATEGY: Identify Emotional Responses

HOW TO IDENTIFY EMOTIONAL RESPONSES

1. **Make a Journal** Jot words and phrases that create a picture in your mind.

2. **Visualize** Focus on the mental images. How do they make you feel?

3. **Respond** Describe your emotional responses.

A. Read the passage. Use the strategies above to identify emotional responses as you read. Then answer the questions.

Look Into the Text

June 28, 1965

Dear Helen,

In my mind I can still see you clearly, standing for hours talking to the students and answering their questions. The questions were not always the most intelligent ones. For instance: "How can you ride horseback when you can't see where the horse is going?" But you gave a wonderful answer. "I just hold onto the horse and let him run wherever he wishes!" And you and the children had a good laugh over this description. Or when you said that after you had learned to speak, you became a real blabbermouth!

1. What words and phrases from the passage helped you create a picture in your mind?

   Answers will vary. _____

   _____

   _____

2. Describe your emotional responses as you read the passage.

   Answers will vary. _____

   _____

   _____

Selection Review To Helen Keller

EQ **What Do You Do to Make an Impression?**
Meet people who are or who want to be unforgettable.

A. In "To Helen Keller," you read two writers' impressions of her. Complete the T Chart with the writers' descriptions of her.

T Chart

Ernst Papanek	Langston Hughes
"How your face expressed your feelings. And how your love inspired the children to carry on . . ."	Within herself, / Found loveliness
"It was unforgettable and moving to see you touch the face of a blind child or kiss the face of a crippled one."	And now the world receives / From her dower
	The message of the strength / Of inner power
"You pushed them in the direction of a happier life."	
"It doesn't sound good enough when I say this. But thank you for what you did for those children, and for all mankind. . . ."	

B. Use the information in the chart to answer the questions.

1. Compare the writers' descriptions of Keller. How are their writing styles similar? How are they different?

   Possible response: Their descriptions are positive and passionate. Papanek's style is familiar. It is obvious that he knows her because he writes his thoughts directly to her. Hughes' style is more formal and dramatic. Both writers use simple words to describe their feelings about her.

2. How did Helen Keller inspire both writers? Use **inspire** in your answer.

   Possible response: Keller inspired the writers because, in spite of huge obstacles, she continued to help others.

3. Why do you think Keller is so unforgettable to so many people?

   Possible response: Keller really listened to people and wanted to help them. She made people feel special and inspired them to make their lives better.

Connect Across Texts

Helen Keller made a strong impression on those around her. Read how these two poets feel about making a mark in the world.

Marked

by Carmen Tafolla

Never write with pencil,
m'ija
It is for those
who would
5   erase.
Make your mark proud
        and open,
Brave,
        beauty folded into
10   its imperfection,
Like a piece of turquoise
        marked.

Never write
with pencil,
15   m'ija.
Write with ink
        or mud,
or berries grown in
gardens never owned,
20   or, sometimes,
     if necessary,
        blood.

Clearing the bark from sticks and arranging it in swirling patterns, 2003, Strijdom van der Merwe. Land art/photo documentation, Kamiyama, Tokushima, Japan.

Key Vocabulary
imperfection *n.*, defect, problem

Interact with the Text

1. Assess Emotional Responses
Underline the command the speaker gives her daughter. What do you picture? How does it make you feel?

Possible response: It makes me picture a proud mother giving her daughter advice about the world. It makes me feel strong, as if the poet is proud of what I can do and be.

2. Figurative Language in Poetry
Circle the simile. What two things does it compare?

Possible response: The simile compares how people can leave a mark on the world with their actions, just like nature leaves its mark on a piece of turquoise.

About the Writer

Carmen Tafolla (1951–   ) grew up in San Antonio, Texas, and started writing poetry when she was a teen. She still lives in San Antonio, in a century-old house with her husband and mother. Tafolla writes fiction as well as poetry. She is also a professor and a public speaker.

3. Figurative Language in Poetry

In your own words, explain what the simile in line 5 means.

Possible response:

When you study music,

you have to practice.

The speaker practices

her writing because she

wants to be really good

at it.

4. Assess Emotional Responses

How does the poet want the reader to feel about her mother?

Possible response: The

poet wants the reader

to see how practical her

mother is. The mother

doesn't understand her

daughter's creativity. Her

mother only sees the

dust.

Dusting

by Julia Alvarez

Each morning I wrote my name
on the dusty cabinet, then crossed
the dining table in script, scrawled
in capitals on the backs of chairs,
5   practicing signatures like scales
while Mother followed, squirting
linseed from a burping can
into a crumpled-up flannel.

In Other Words
scrawled wrote
scales music notes played for practice
linseed furniture polish
flannel cloth

She erased my fingerprints
10   from the bookshelf and rocker,

polished mirrors on the desk

scribbled with my alphabets.

My name was swallowed in the towel

with which she jeweled the table tops.

15   The grain surfaced in the oak

and the pine grew luminous.

But I refused with every mark

to be like her, anonymous. ❖

About the Writer

Julia Alvarez (1950–) is the author of many novels and books of poetry. Her family moved from the Dominican Republic to New York when she was ten. Alvarez believes that learning English helped her become a writer. "I had to pay close attention to each word," she says.

Key Vocabulary
anonymous *adj.*, unknown, unnamed

5. Assess Emotional Responses

Think about the images the poet creates. What is your emotional response to these images?

Possible response:

I picture a person's

ideas being erased.

It makes me feel sad

for her because she is

trying to make her mark

and create something

beautiful.

6. Interpret

What does the poet say she does not want to be like? What can you conclude about the poet?

Possible response: The

poet does not want to be

anonymous. She wants

to share her art and

ideas with the world.

Selection Review Marked/Dusting

A. Complete the chart with examples of figurative language from the poems.

Types of Figurative Language	Examples from the Texts
Simile	"Like a piece of turquoise marked"
Personification	"a burping can" "My name was swallowed in the towel / with which she jeweled the table tops."
Symbol	a pencil marks in dust berries grown in gardens never owned blood

B. Answer the questions.

1. Choose one example of figurative language from the chart in Activity A. Describe what image the words create in your mind. What responses do you have to the speaker's words and ideas?

Answers will vary.

_____

_____

_____

_____

_____

2. How would each poet describe the other's idea of making an impression?

Answers will vary.

_____

_____

_____

_____

_____

Reflect and Assess

WRITING: Write About Literature

A. Plan your writing. List details and ideas from each selection that show how someone can "make a mark." *Answers will vary.*

To Helen Keller	Marked/Dusting
Helen Keller made a mark by being patient, even when people asked questions that were unintelligent or rude.	You can make a mark by being proud of who you are and what you believe.

B. Write a short poem to express your feelings and thoughts about how people can "make a mark." Use details and ideas from each selection to write your poem.

Students should clearly show how each selection is represented in their poems.

_____

_____

_____

_____

_____

_____

_____

_____

_____

_____

_____

Integrate the Language Arts

LITERARY ANALYSIS: Analyze Alliteration and Consonance

Alliteration is the repetition of consonant sounds at the beginnings of words. **Consonance** is the repetition of consonant sounds within a line or verse of a poem.

Example of alliteration: **s**ignatures like **s**cales
Example of consonance: scri**bb**led with my alpha**b**ets

A. Find examples of alliteration from either "Marked" or from "Dusting." List the examples below. Then underline the repeated sound.

1. Make your mark proud

2. Brave, beauty

3. on the dusty cabinet, then crossed

4. the dining table in script, scrawled

5. practicing signatures like scales.

B. Write a line of alliteration for each sound listed below. *Answers will vary.*

1. *th* _____

2. *ch* _____

3. *dr* _____

4. *fr* _____

5. *scr* _____

C. Write a short poem using either alliteration or consonance. Use the lines you wrote in Activity B, if necessary.

Answers will vary.

_____

_____

_____

_____

_____

_____

_____

_____

_____

_____

_____

_____

_____

VOCABULARY STUDY: Connotation and Denotation

Denotation is the literal, or precise, meaning of a word. **Connotation** is the feeling or idea that a word suggests.

A. Circle the word in each pair that has a more positive connotation.

Word Pairs	
1. scribble / (write)	5. (encourage) / insist
2. (walk) / stalk	6. exaggerate / (embellish)
3. stingy / (frugal)	7. (wander) / drift
4. noisy / (loud)	8. steal / (take)

B. Read the words in the chart below and list the connotation and denotation for each word. *Answers will vary. Possible responses are shown.*

Word	Denotation	Connotation
embellish	to add beauty to	adding more detail
exaggerate	to say or think something is larger than it is	misleading; somewhat false
frugal	without waste	careful with your spending
stingy	unwilling to spend or give money	hoarding, greedy

C. Use each of the words below in a sentence. Ask a partner to tell you if you have used the word with a positive or negative connotation. *Answers will vary.*

1. stingy _____

_____

2. frugal _____

_____

3. exaggerate _____

_____

4. embellish _____

_____

Key Vocabulary Review

A. Use the words to complete the paragraph.

anonymous	desire	personality	romantic
compliment	nervous	reveal	unforgettable

One day Rebecca found an ___anonymous___ (1) letter in her locker. The boy who wrote it must have been

too ___nervous___ (2), or shy, to ___reveal___ (3) his identity. He was very ___romantic___ (4), and

he expressed his ___desire___ (5) to go out on a date with her. He gave her a ___compliment___ (6) and

said he thought she had a nice ___personality___ (7). Rebecca said the letter was ___unforgettable___ (8) and

that she would always keep it.

B. Use your own words to write what each Key Vocabulary word means.
Then write a synonym for each word. *Answers will vary. Possible responses are shown.*

Key Word	My Definition	Synonym
1. conceal	to cover something up	hide
2. conquer	to beat something	defeat
3. contribute	to help or be a part of	assist or give
4. elegance	something that has high quality or beauty	good taste
5. horizon	where the earth meets the sky	skyline
6. overcome	to solve	beat
7. privacy	being away from others	solitude
8. recover	to return to the original state	restore